CREATING ART

Lessons & Projects for the Grammar Stage

Lori Schloemer

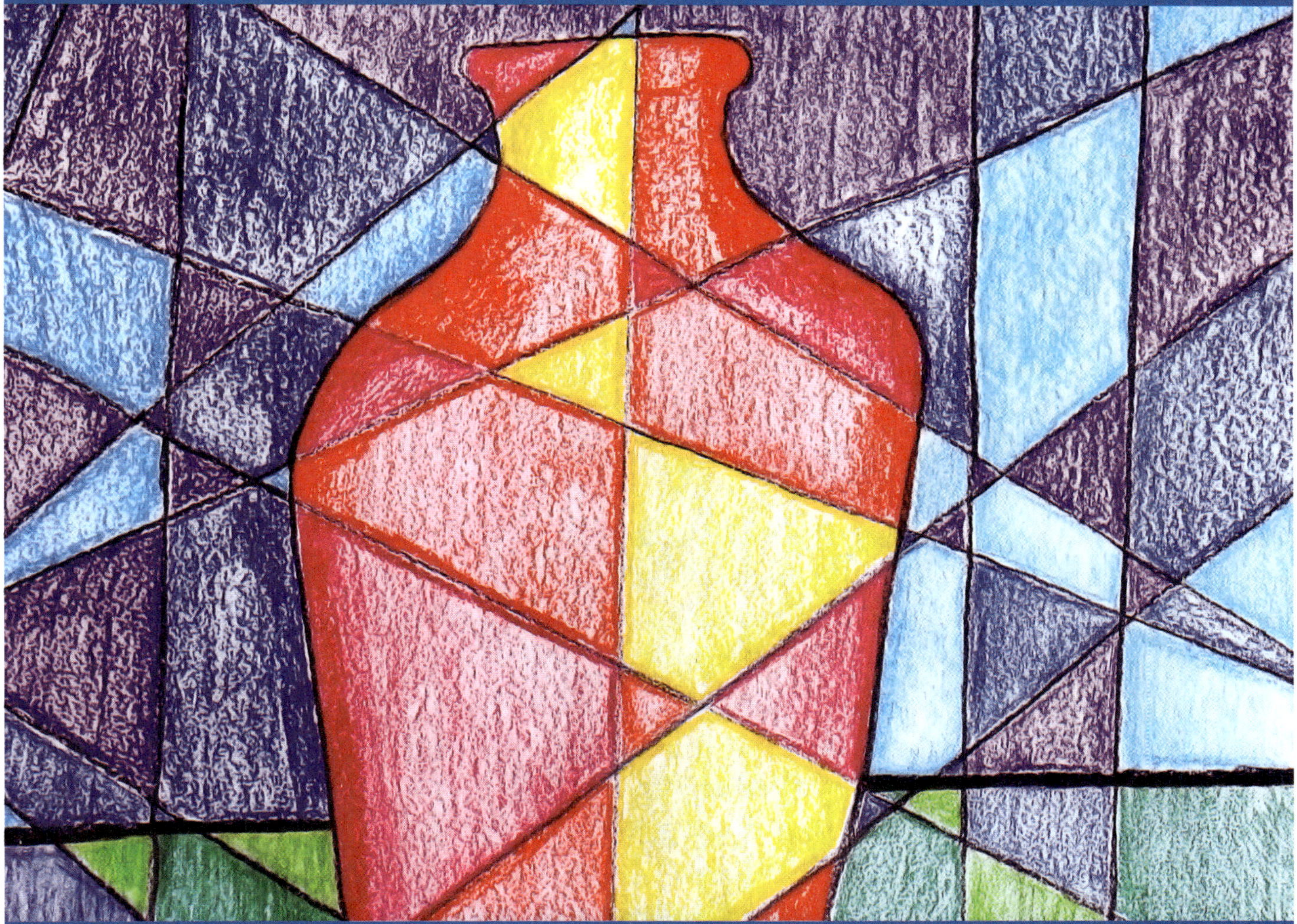

MEMORIA PRESS

MEMORIA PRESS
www.MemoriaPress.com

CREATING ART
Lessons & Projects for the Grammar Stage

Lori Schloemer

ISBN 978-1-61538-601-7

Illustrated by Jessica Osborne

CONTENTS

Thank you for choosing the Memoria Press 3rd Grade Art Curriculum for your student or class. This curriculum is designed to challenge students as they develop a strong work ethic, an appreciation for art, and a higher level of mastery. Students will begin with color theory, walk through a brief period of history, and encounter a general reinforcement of the Memoria Press 3rd Grade Curriculum, particularly in the subjects of science and literature.

NOTES TO THE TEACHER

This Teacher Guide is intended to be used for a 30-45 minute classroom setting, approximately 10-15 students, but can be modified for individual use. Each lesson is meant to build on a foundation, from which students should be able to refer to and apply to future lessons. The goal of this class is to build an understanding of general color theory and basic art techniques, as well as a beginning knowledge of early art history, and a reinforcement of the Memoria Press 3rd Grade Curriculum. Use of the Teacher Guide will be most beneficial when the terms are used in the classroom discussions and explanations.

Each class and/or student works at various paces, thus you as the teacher must adjust the pace and time given to each lesson to that which suits your circumstance. Keep in mind the following factors: class size, number of meetings within the week or month, time allowed for projects, lectures, and quizzes. The quizzes allow you to develop your own class structure, as well as assess terms and understanding. (Quizzes are optional and are located at the end of the guide.)

PREPARATION AND INSTRUCTION:

- Read through the notes and instructions for each lesson.
- Prepare an example to show your student or class. This will also help you to understand the techniques and steps of the project.
- Know the vocabulary and be able to discuss the terms.

GRADING:

Grading art is subjective, thus grading should be assessed in the following areas:

- Participation in class
- Effort
- Completion
- Attitude
- Fulfillment of all necessary elements required per project

MATERIALS NEEDED

- [ ] 8.5″ x 11″ white card stock
- [ ] 8.5″ x 11″ white paper
- [ ] 11″ x 17″ white card stock or paint-grade paper
- [ ] 11″ x 17″ black paper
- [ ] Acrylic or tempera paint in red, yellow, blue, brown, black, and white*
- [ ] butcher paper
- [ ] Chalk in brown, black, white, red, and yellow
- [ ] Colored pencils
- [ ] Construction paper
- [ ] Decoupage glue
- [ ] Glow-in-the-dark paint
- [ ] Glue
- [ ] Glue stick
- [ ] Hole puncher
- [ ] Markers
- [ ] Mixing tray
- [ ] Paintbrushes
- [ ] Paper plate
- [ ] Pencils
- [ ] Piece of plastic fruit
- [ ] Ruler
- [ ] Scissors
- [ ] Styrofoam Easter eggs (or papier-mâché eggs)
- [ ] Tissue paper (multiple colors)
- [ ] Toothpicks
- [ ] Vase
- [ ] Watercolor paints
- [ ] White crayons (you can also use light yellow)
- [ ] Wooden skewers
- [ ] Yarn

*For lessons that do not specify the type of paint, you may use acrylic or tempera.

LESSON 1: Introduction to Color Theory

TERMS TO KNOW

Visual Spectrum — The range of wavelengths the human eye can see

Primary Colors — Colors that cannot be made by mixing other colors: red, yellow, and blue

Secondary Colors — Colors that are made by mixing two primary colors: orange, green, and violet (purple)

GENERAL FACTS

1. The colors we see with our eyes are part of the visible spectrum. The visible spectrum is made up of waves of reflected light, which vary in length.
2. Each wavelength allows us to see a different color.
3. The longest wavelength is red.
4. The shortest wavelength is violet (purple).
5. When referring to the visible spectrum, black is not a color because black is the absence of light.

ACTIVITIES

1. Turn out all the lights and ask the students: "If the visible spectrum is made up of wavelengths of light, and I take away all the light, what can you see?"
   Nothing, or blackness; therefore, black is the absence of color (or light).
2. Using a prism and natural light, show a rainbow of light and have the children identify the colors they see.

QUESTIONS

1. Where can we see the entire visible spectrum all at once?
   A rainbow
2. What are the primary colors?
   Red, yellow, and blue
3. Why are they called primary colors?
   Because they cannot be made by mixing other colors.
4. What are the secondary colors?
   Orange, green, and purple
5. How are secondary colors made?
   By mixing two primary colors together.

PROJECT 1: Color Wheel Using Primary and Secondary Colors

MATERIALS NEEDED

- ☐ 8.5″ x 11″ sheet of white paper
- ☐ Pencil
- ☐ Ruler
- ☐ Glue stick
- ☐ 1″x 1″ square of each color: red, orange, yellow, green, blue, and purple

INSTRUCTIONS

1. Using your ruler and pencil, draw a vertical line approximately 5″ long in the center of the paper. Draw 2 lines approximately 5″ long on the diagonal through the center point, allowing equal space for the color squares.
2. Using your glue stick, glue the color squares in rainbow order, starting at the tip of the first line and going in a clockwise direction.

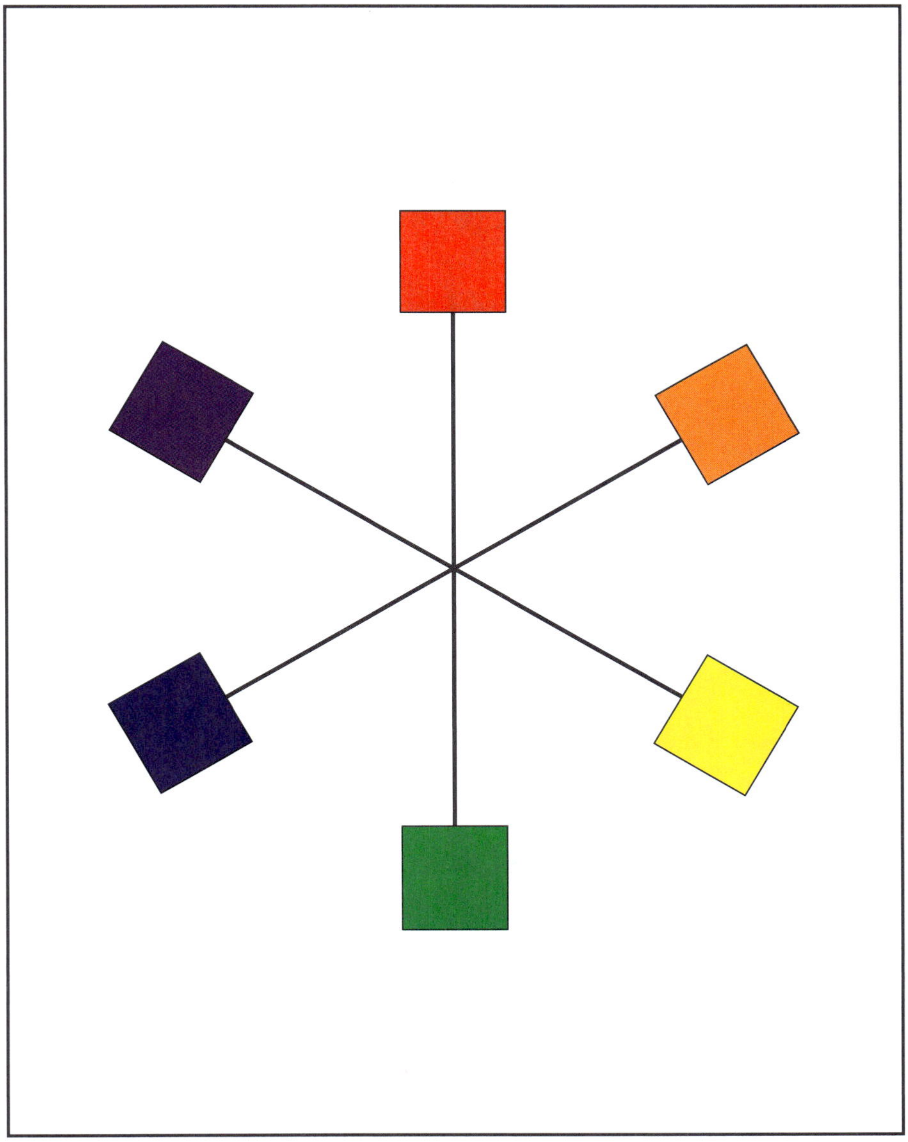

PROJECT 1A:
Painted Color Wheel Using Primary and Secondary Colors

MATERIALS NEEDED

- ☐ Color Wheel template printed on 8.5″ x 11″ card stock
- ☐ Acrylic or tempera paint in primary colors (red, yellow, blue)*
- ☐ Paintbrush
- ☐ Mixing tray
- ☐ Water

*Colored pencils may be used to color in the wheel if paint is not available.

INSTRUCTIONS

1. Begin by coloring or painting the inner circle with primary colors. R = red, Y = yellow, B = blue.
2. Next, use the primary colors to explain how secondary colors are created. Mix together R and Y to create O (O = Orange). Notice that on the wheel the secondary colors are in the second ring. Paint in the area labeled "O."
3. Next, mix Y and B to create G (G = Green), and fill in the designated section on the second ring.
4. Last, mix B and R to create V (V = Violet). Be sure to explain that violet is another name for purple.
5. Remember to keep these paintings for the next lesson, as you will be adding to them.

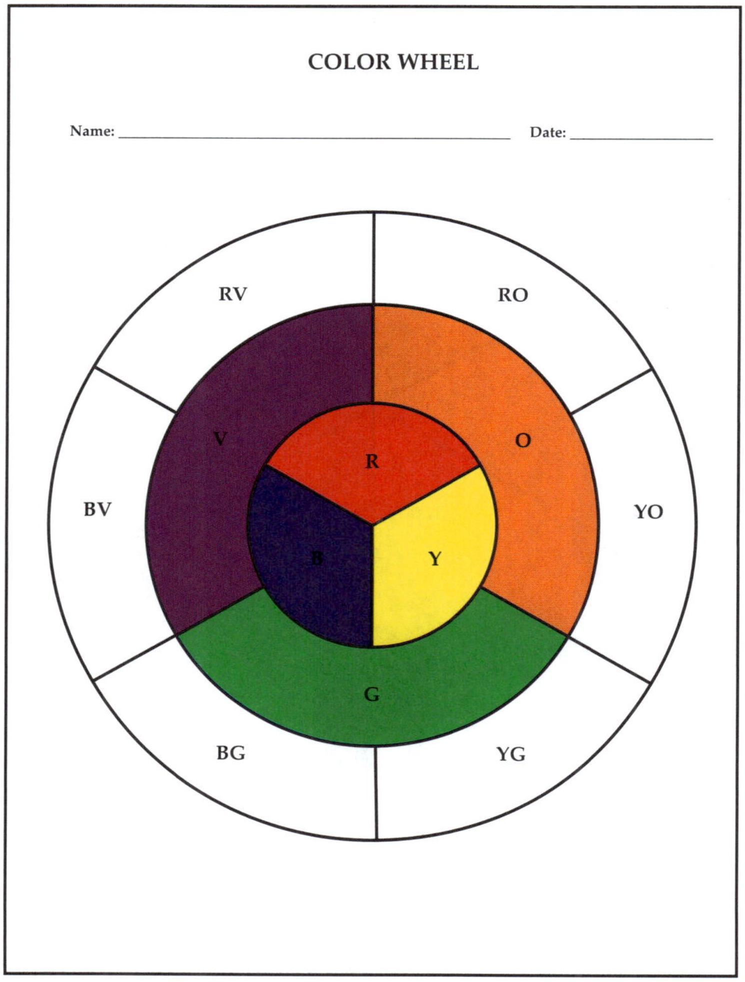

LESSON 2: Color Theory Continued

REVIEW

1. What are the wavelengths of light we can see called?
   Visible spectrum
2. What color is the shortest wavelength of light?
   Purple
3. What color is the longest wavelength of light?
   Red
4. What are the primary colors?
   Red, yellow, blue
5. What are the secondary colors?
   Orange, green, purple
6. How do we get secondary colors?
   By mixing two primary colors

TERMS TO KNOW

Tertiary Color — A color created by mixing together one primary and one adjacent secondary color

Hue — A color in its natural state, as found on the color wheel

Tint — A natural color to which white has been added to lighten it

Shade — A natural color to which black has been added to darken it

Key Color — Main or predominant color within a project or a piece of art

Color Scheme — A fixed relationship between colors and their position on the color wheel

GENERAL FACTS

1. There is a third group of colors, called tertiary colors.
2. Tertiary colors are made by mixing together a primary and a secondary color.
3. The tertiary colors are red-orange, yellow-orange, yellow-green, blue-green, blue-violet, and red-violet.
4. When naming the tertiary colors, the primary color is listed first.
5. Primary, secondary, and tertiary colors may be used together to create **color schemes**.

COLOR SCHEMES: Have your students use their color wheels during the explanation of this section, or provide them with a new copy of the color wheel from the previous lesson.

Monochromatic Color Scheme — Using only tints and/or shades of one color to create a project or art piece

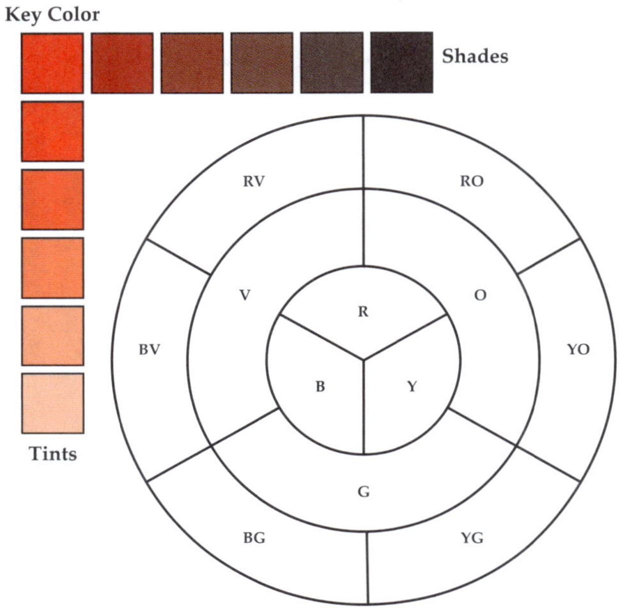

Complementary Color Scheme — Using colors that are directly across from each other on the color wheel: red/green, blue/orange, yellow/violet (purple)

Every primary color has a secondary color as a complement.

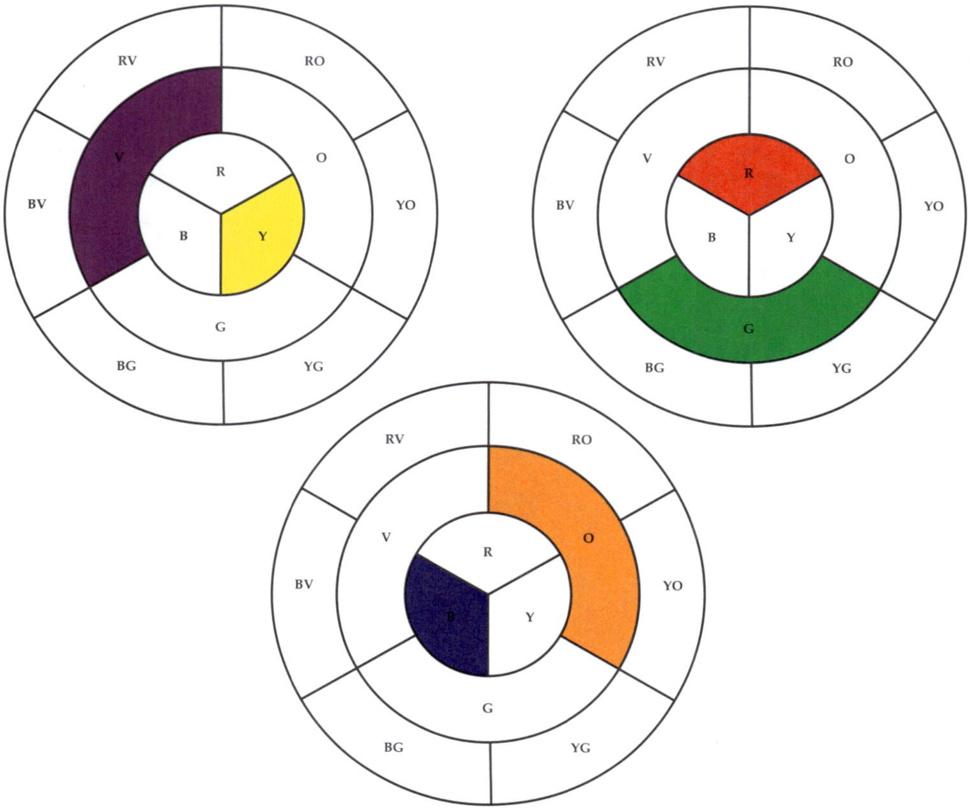

Analogous Color Scheme — Using a minimum of two, but no more than five, colors that are adjacent (in a row) on the color wheel. Typically, three colors are used. An example is: R, RO, O.

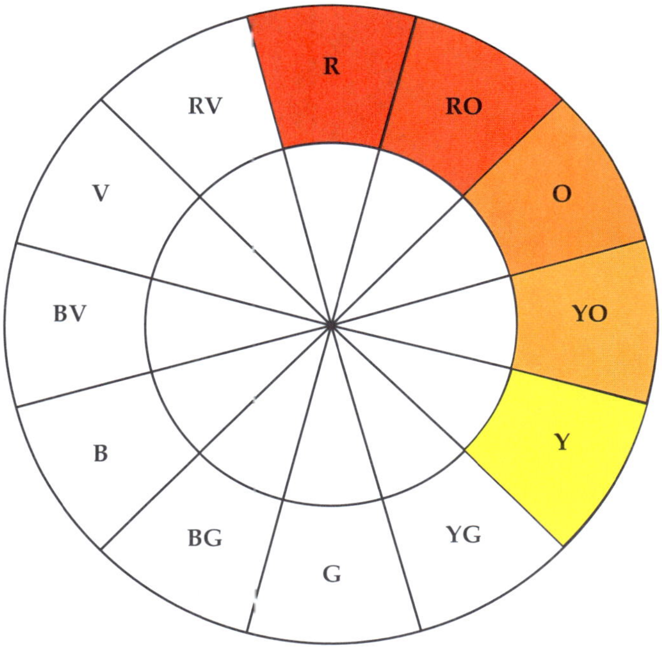

Triad Color Scheme — Using three colors equally spaced on the color wheel

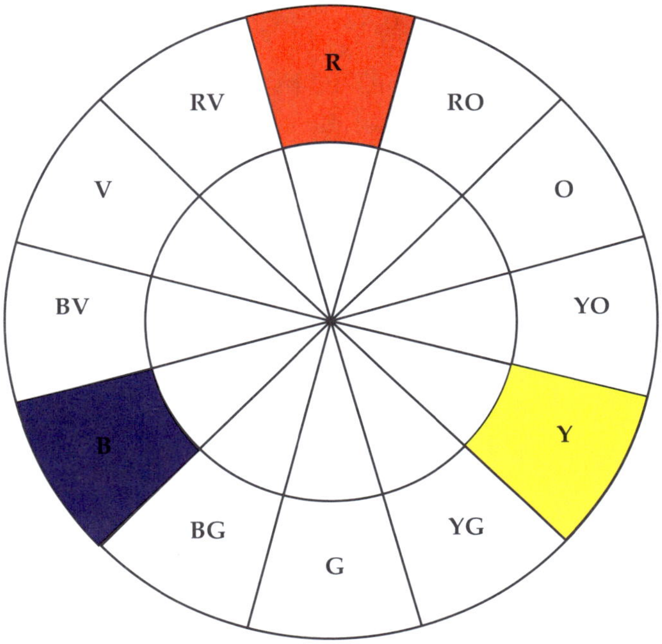

Split Complementary Color Scheme — Using two colors directly adjacent (on either side of) to the complement of the key color. Example: If red is the key color, then its complement is green and the split complementary color scheme is: R, YG, BG.

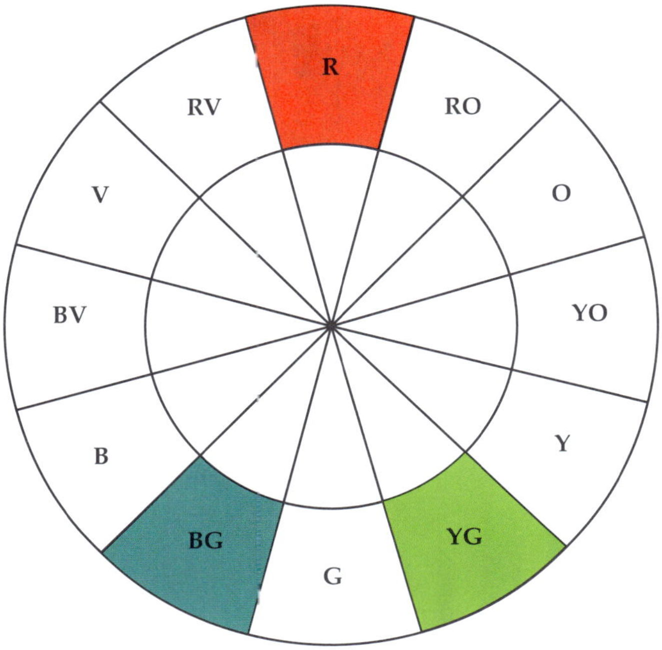

PROJECT 2: Color Schemes

MATERIALS NEEDED

- ☐ Student color wheel (as a reference)
- ☐ 8.5″ x 11″ white paper
- ☐ Colored pencils
- ☐ Ruler
- ☐ Pencil

*This project could also be done using paint on chipboard or card stock.

INSTRUCTIONS

1. Have students choose from triangles, rectangles, or squares. Next, have students choose a complementary color scheme. Using the chosen shape, have students draw their shape six times on the paper following these rules:
   - Every shape has to overlap at least one other shape.
   - Shapes may vary in size, as long as they stay on the page.
   - Shapes are to change directions.
2. Notice that by layering the shapes, you have created new shapes. Have students color in the original shapes and the created shapes using their chosen color scheme following these rules:
   - Use the two colors from your chosen complementary color scheme and any of their tints or shades. This is accomplished by coloring a shape in its hue, then coloring over it lightly with white or black.
   - No two shapes of the same color may touch on a straight line. (Using purple, a purple triangle may touch purple on the point but not on a shared line. When you allow two shapes to touch on a shared line, it combines the two shapes and the design of the project gets lost.)

****It is important to have the students constantly change colors so that they do not end up with two shapes the same color that touch on a straight line. This is a common mistake as students will try to color in five shapes of purple at once, then end up blending two shapes into one. If a student has two shapes that touch on a straight line, use black or white to change the hue to a shade or tint, thus keeping the integrity of the design.****

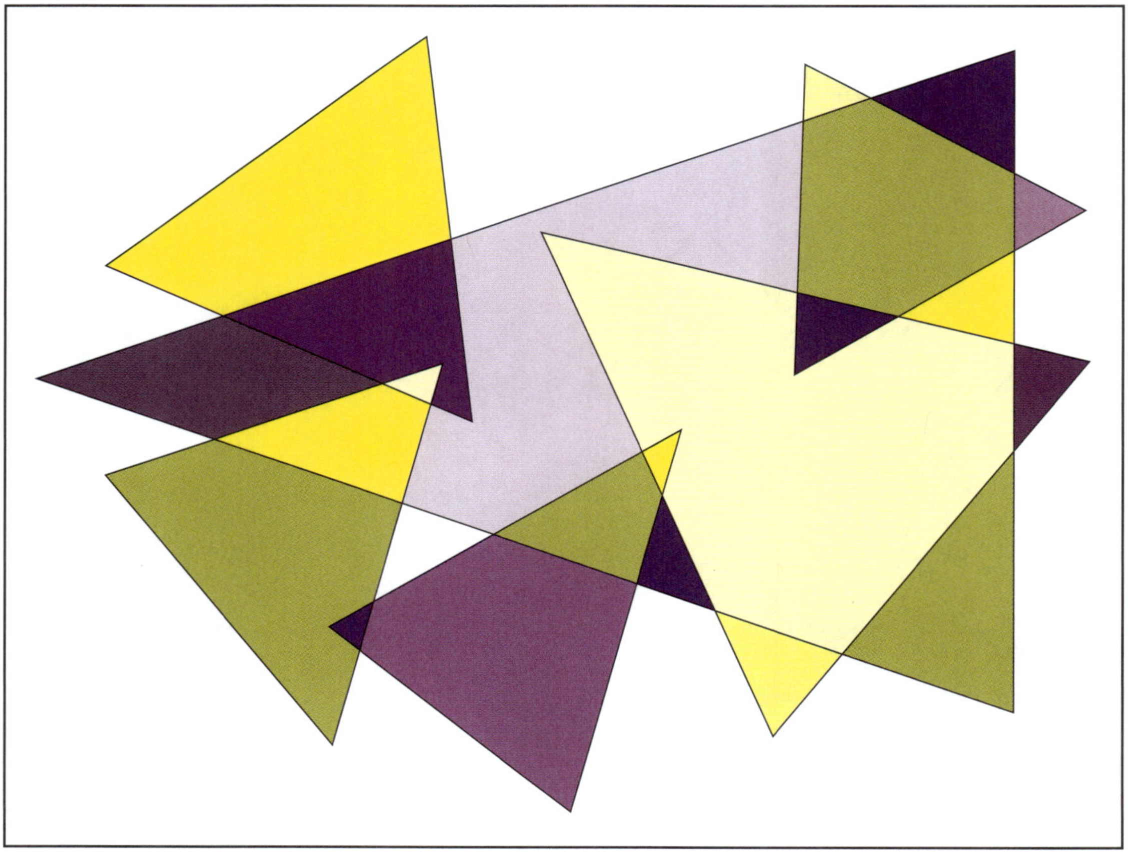

☐ **Option 1:** Have the students put a black horizontal curvilinear line through the design to add line contrast. See example below. (Note: The curvilinear line creates additional abnormal shapes that must not share colors.)

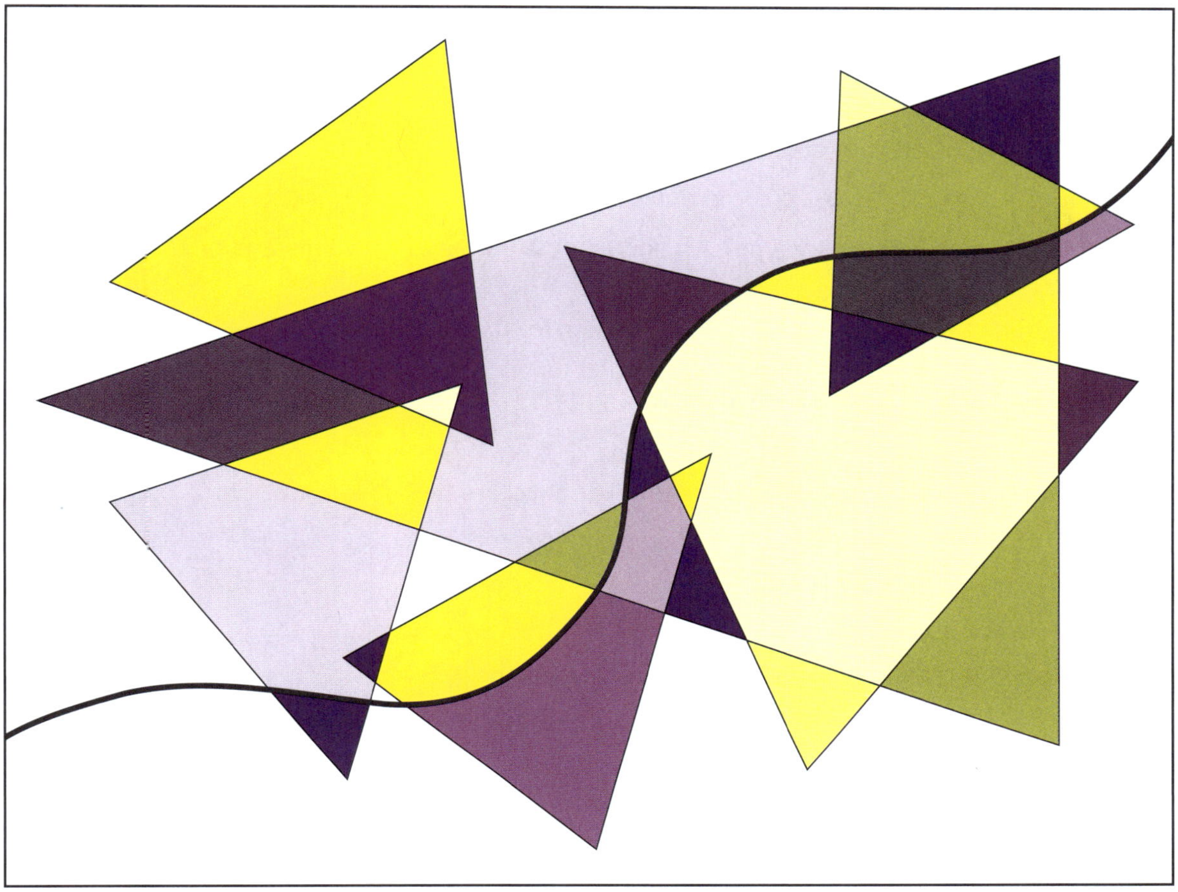

☐ **Option 2:** If time permits or students finish their project early, have them start another project using a different shape and complementary color scheme.

LESSON 3: Line Direction, Texture, and Value

REVIEW

1. What color is the longest wavelength of light? Red
2. What are the primary colors? Red, yellow, blue
3. What is a tint? Adding white to a color to lighten it.
4. What is a shade? Adding black to a color to darken it.
5. What is a monochromatic color scheme? A color scheme that uses only tints and/or shades of one color.
6. What is a complementary color scheme?
   A color scheme that uses colors that are directly across from each other on the color wheel: red/green, blue/orange, yellow/violet (purple).

TERMS TO KNOW

Contrast — The distinction between light colors and dark colors

Value — The relative lightness or darkness of a color; also referred to as **gray scale**

Line types:

» ***Continuous*** — A solid line

» ***Zigzag*** — A combination of diagonal lines that connect at each point

» ***Dotted or Dashed*** — A line that is broken into segments or patterns

» ***Curvy*** — A line with soft bends and no angles

Textures:

» ***Continuous*** — A pattern or image created with smooth, uninterrupted lines (without picking up the pencil, pen, or brush to break the line at any point)

» ***Stipple/Dot*** — A pattern or image created with dots

» ***Crosshatch*** — Parallel lines that intersect each other, used to shade or mark an image

» ***Blending/Gradation*** — A gentle and gradual transition from dark to light

PROJECT 3: Value Scales

MATERIALS NEEDED

- ☐ 8.5″ x 11″ white card stock
- ☐ Ruler
- ☐ Pencil
- ☐ Paint – white and black
- ☐ Paintbrushes
- ☐ Mixing tray

INSTRUCTIONS

1. Have students position their paper in a horizontal, or landscape, position. Next, have students draw ten 1″ squares in a row. (See example below.)
2. Starting at the left end, have students paint the first square white. Add one drop of black paint to the white paint and mix it well. Have the students paint the second square. Continue this process until all the squares are painted, each time adding only one drop of black paint.
3. As students paint each square, it is important to explain that they are creating values of white, or a value scale, also known as a gray scale. It is also important to remember that each student may end up with different values based on the amount of white paint each one started with.
4. This project will also help students learn how to draw and measure using a ruler or straight edge.

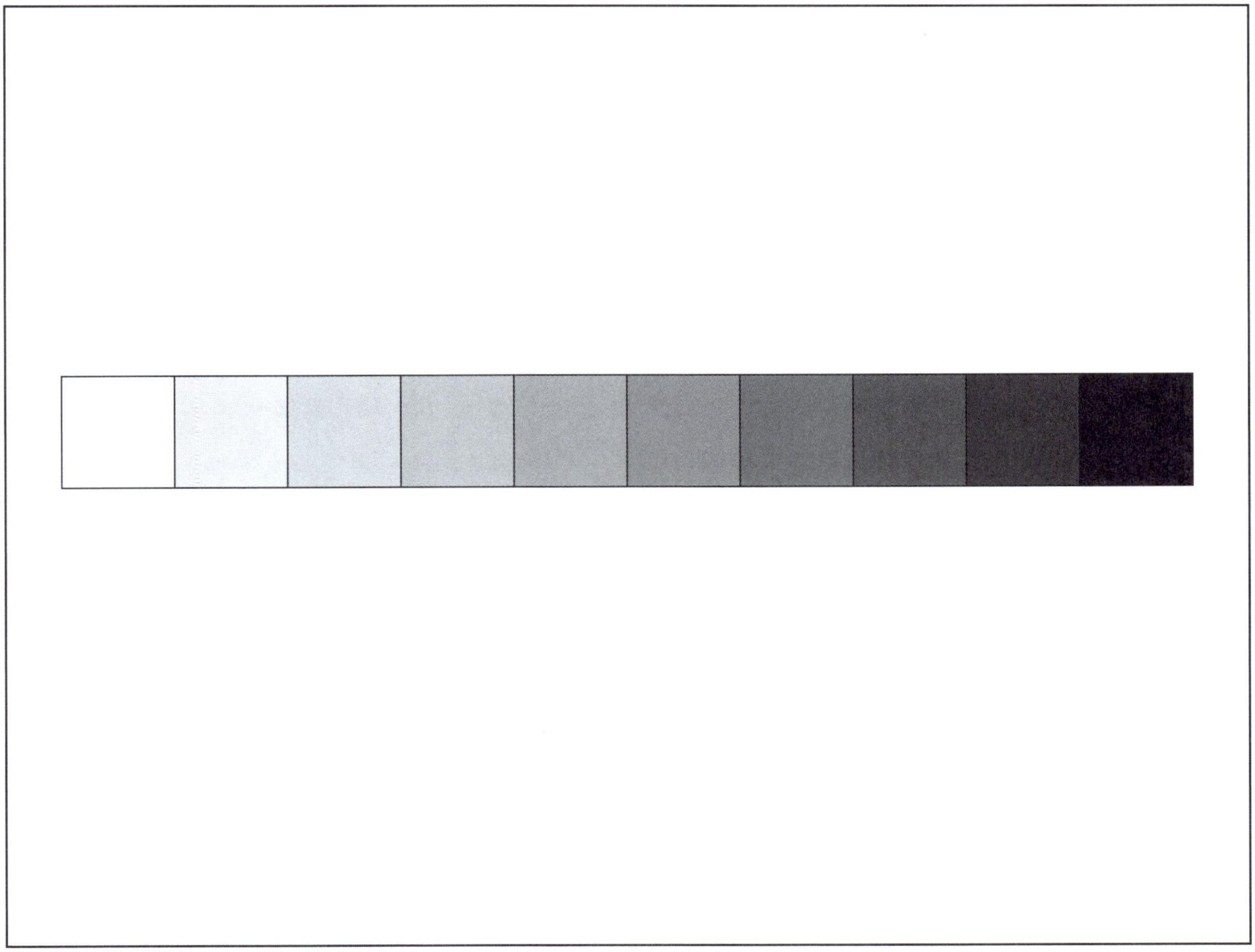

PROJECT 3A: Value Scales

MATERIALS NEEDED

- ☐ 8.5″ x 11″ white card stock
- ☐ Ruler
- ☐ Pencil
- ☐ Paint – white and one additional color of choice
- ☐ Paintbrushes
- ☐ Mixing tray

*This project could also be used to reinforce primary and/or secondary colors by having the students complete a value scale for each, or for any of the color schemes previously mentioned in Lesson 2.

INSTRUCTIONS

1. Have students position their paper in a horizontal, or landscape, position. Next, have students draw ten 1″squares in a row.
2. Starting at the left end, have students paint the first square white. Add one drop of the chosen paint to the white paint and mix it well. Have the students paint the second square. Continue this process until all the squares are painted, each time only adding one drop of the same chosen paint.
3. As you paint each square, it is important to explain that you are creating values of white, or a value scale, also known as a color scale. It is also important to remember that each student may end up with different values, based on the amount of white paint each one started with.

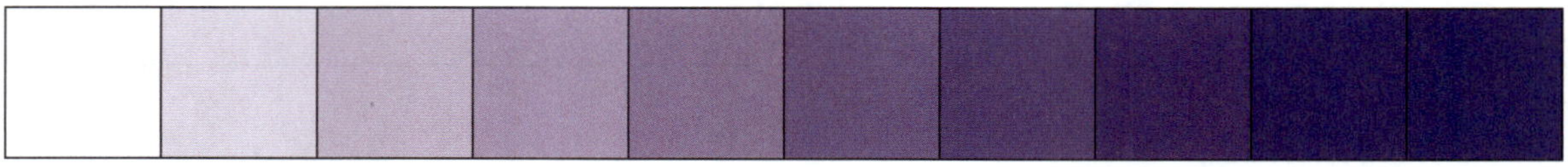

4. In addition, you may want to have the students start with the key color, or color of choice, and add one drop of white each time. Next, have them repeat the process, starting with the same key color and add black. This would allow them to see the difference between tints and shades of that particular color. It would also help them to understand the relationship between values, tints, and shades.

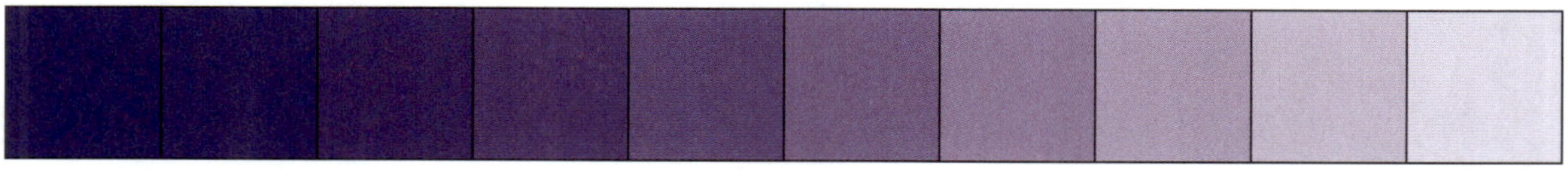

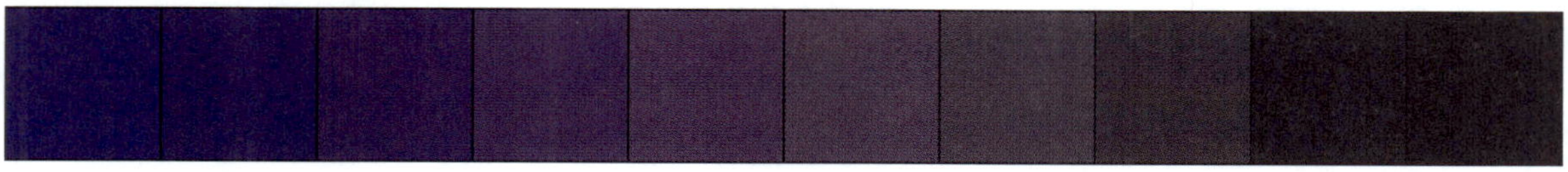

SPECIAL PROJECT 1: Monochromatic Pumpkins

REVIEW

Analogous Color Scheme — A color scheme that uses a minimum of two, but no more than five, colors that are adjacent (in a row) on the color wheel

MATERIALS NEEDED

- ☐ Orange paint
- ☐ Black paint
- ☐ White paint
- ☐ 8.5″ x 11″ white card stock
- ☐ Paintbrushes

INSTRUCTIONS

1. Have the students use orange paint to paint a pumpkin shape in the center of the piece of card stock. You may describe it as an oval with two small horizontal bumps near the top.

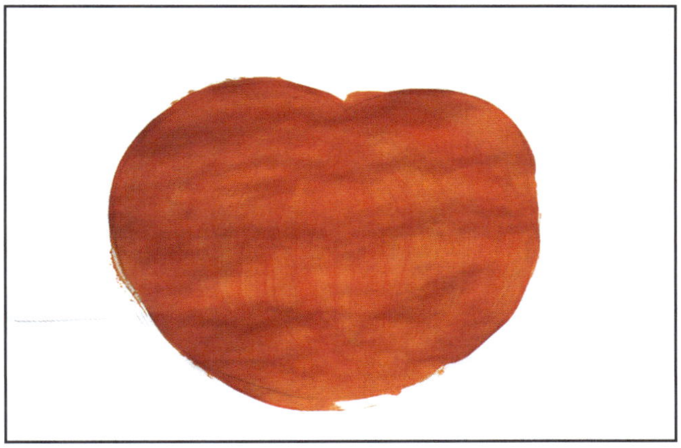

2. Next, have students mix a small amount of black paint with some orange paint to create a shade. Instruct them to use the shade to paint the soft texture of the pumpkin surface. They will be painting over the original orange pumpkin shape. This technique is called a wet-on-wet technique; the paint will blend and create new shades. Be sure the students do not cover up the entire original orange pumpkin shape and are following the contour of the pumpkin, painting in a vertical direction.

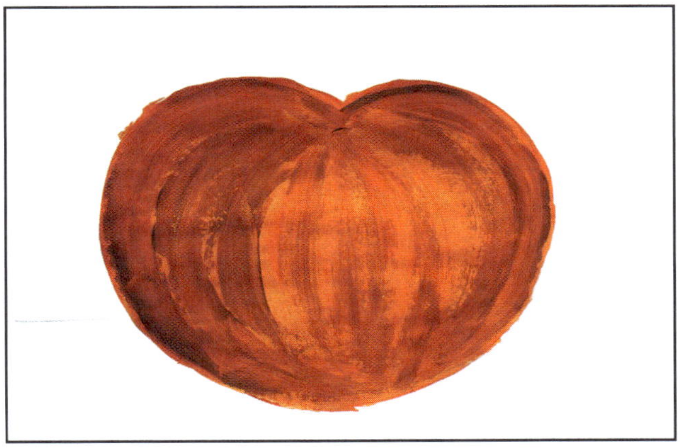

3. Have the students use black paint to make a thin outline, starting at the top of the pumpkin, around the edge, that fades out toward the bottom. Next, have them draw three black lines that are short and fade, following the contour of the pumpkin, on the left and right sides to give the pumpkin a three-dimensional appearance. Last, have them make one very short vertical black line in the center. Next, with a clean brush, using white paint, have them outline the three black lines on the right. These are highlights, reflections created by a light source, and should go above the black lines.

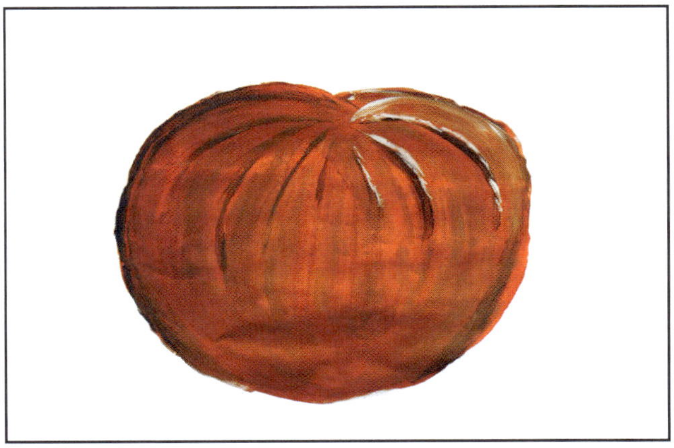

4. Next, have the students mix some black and white paint together to create a dark gray color. Starting to the left of the pumpkin and painting horizontally, create a table line by gently moving the brush back and forth, getting as close as possible to the pumpkin without touching it. They will continue this process until they have gone under the pumpkin and created a table line on the other side. Note: As the students are creating their table, each time they reload the brush with paint, they need to add more white. This creates a lighter surface on the right, which is where the light source is. Point out that they are creating a value scale or gradation by doing this. Remind the students not to go all the way to the edge of the pumpkin. If students do paint over the pumpkin, have them clean their brush and, using just a damp brush, have them re-work the paint on the pumpkin.

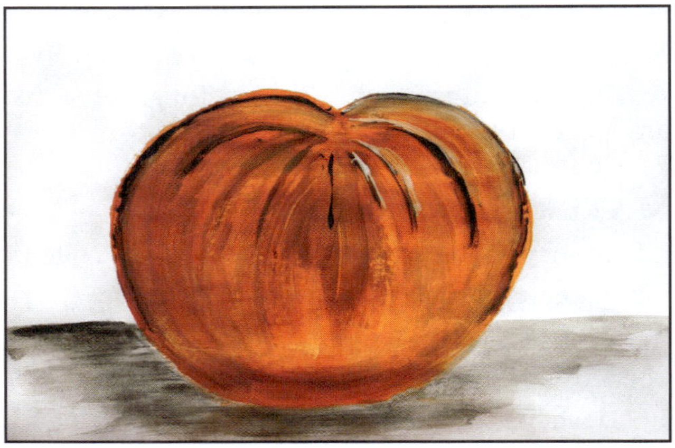

5. Next, have the students clean their brush and get some black paint. They will now paint the stem of the pumpkin. Start by painting a "V" in the middle, where the two bumps of the pumpkin meet. Next, paint in a vertical motion up toward the right. Repeat the process, painting a shorter line up toward the left. Connect the tops of the two vertical lines and fill in the shape. Then clean the brush.

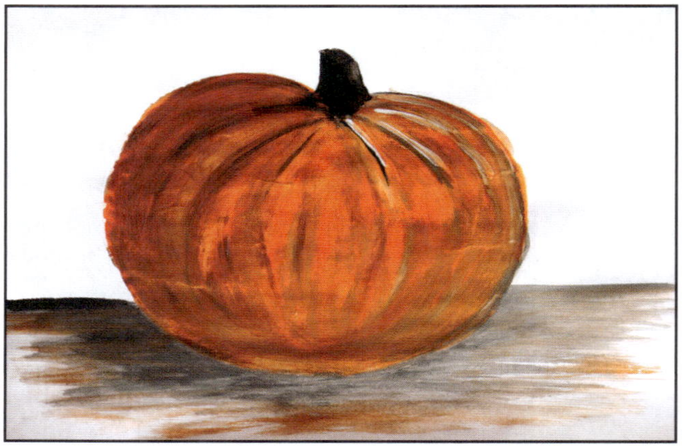

6. While the stem is drying, have the students mix some orange, white, and a small amount of black paint, creating a tone, the process of adding both black and white to a natural color. Add a small amount of water to this mixture to make it more workable. Have students brush this mixture over the horizontal table and extending past it to create a technique call a wash, also adding a three-dimensional aspect. Again, do not go all the way to the edge of the paper.

7. To finish the pumpkin, have the students clean and dry their brushes. Using a very small amount of white paint, have the students create highlights on the stem. To do this, have them make a very thin vertical line on the far right side of the stem. Next, from the top of that line, have them create a "V" shape that dips down and connects to the other side of the stem, which will create a black square. Make one more short white line that starts at the point of the "V" and goes slightly down the center of the stem. If time allows, have the students make a wash with white paint and water and brush a small amount on the two vertical portions of the stem, and on the diagonal in the black square to create texture. (See example below.)

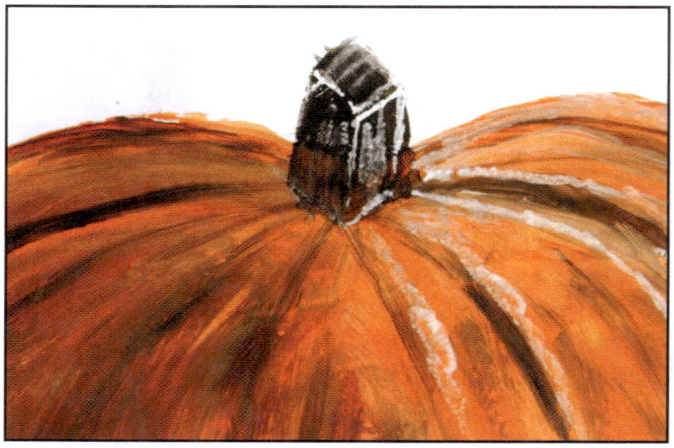

LESSON 4: Portraits

REVIEW

Textures:

» ***Continuous*** — A pattern or image created with smooth, uninterrupted lines (without picking up the pencil, pen, or brush to break the line at any point)

» ***Stipple/Dot*** — A pattern or image created with dots

» ***Crosshatch*** — Parallel lines that intersect each other, used to shade or mark an image

» ***Blending/Gradation*** — A gentle and gradual transition from dark to light

TERMS TO KNOW

Portrait Format — The format used for a portrait; a rectangle that is taller than it is wide

Oval — The space around the subject in a portrait to contain proper proportions. This is not always visible; it is often implied.

Breathing Area — The space outside the oval

GENERAL FACTS

SIZE is determined by the purpose of the portrait

- A **small** portrait is intimate and personal. Reasons:
  - » More portable
  - » Easily displayed
  - » More affordable
- A **large** portrait is authoritative and is a sign of nobility; usually indicates a "god" characteristic or complex. Reasons:
  - » Very costly, affordable only by those with much wealth and social status; designed to be displayed in a large space
  - » To advertise oneself
  - » To be intimidating or appear as if to "lord" over

LENGTH

- **½ length:** usually seated, showing the head, shoulders, and upper chest. (Most common type of portrait.) The knees are not visible or implied.
- **¾ length:** showing from the head to the knees (visible or implied)
- **Full length:** head to toe; subject may be seated or standing

VIEW

Full face: The head and shoulders are facing ***completely*** forward.

¾ view: The face is forward, while shoulders and body are at a slight angle, or vice versa. (most common view)

Profile: The head and body are perpendicular to the viewer.

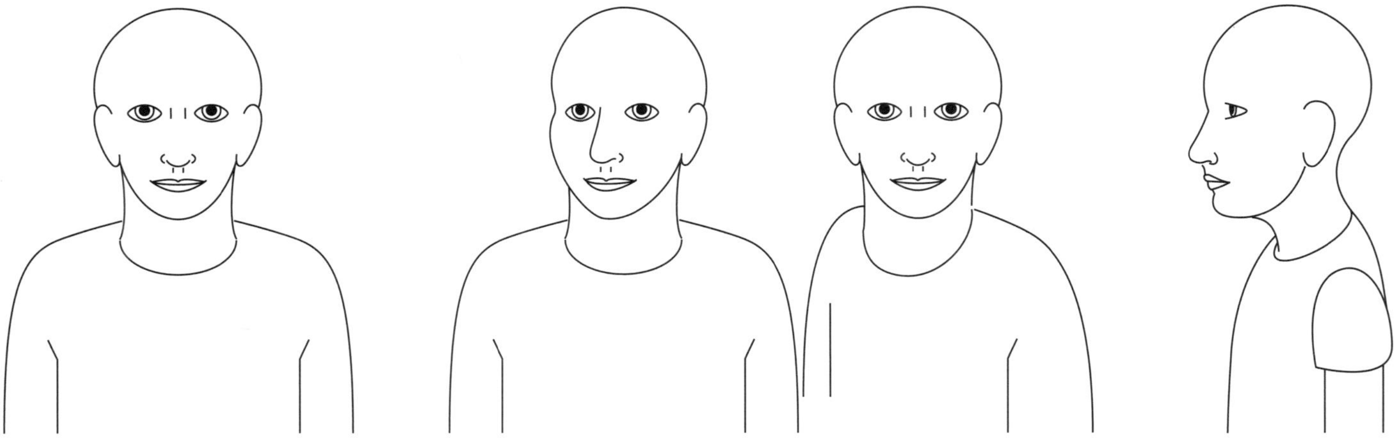

When viewing a portrait, we can learn a lot about the subject from clues in the background or in the clothes they are wearing. For example, abundant, flowing fabric indicates wealth. Objects in the background may help determine the time period or location. Depending on the age of the portrait, the colors may also indicate a region or portion of the world, as pigments were limited by region and environment.

PROJECT 4: Portraits

MATERIALS NEEDED

- ☐ 8.5″ x 11″ white card stock
- ☐ Ruler
- ☐ Pencil

INSTRUCTIONS

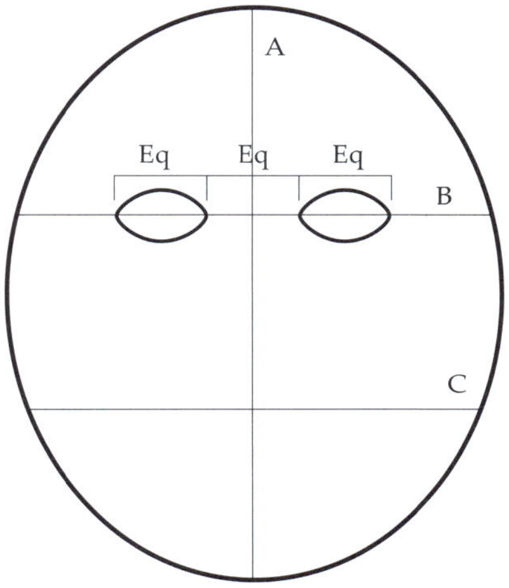

1. Have students start by drawing an oval in the upper half of the page. Draw a faint vertical line down the center of the oval, as indicated to the right, also known as a guideline (see line A). Draw a light horizontal line about 2/3 of the way up on the oval, as shown below; this is line B. Next, draw a third line, horizontal, 1/3 of the way up on the oval and parallel to the second line; this is line C. Line B is for the placement of the eyes. Eyes are drawn in the shape of lemons. The distance between the eyes is equal to the size of one eye (see diagram to the right).

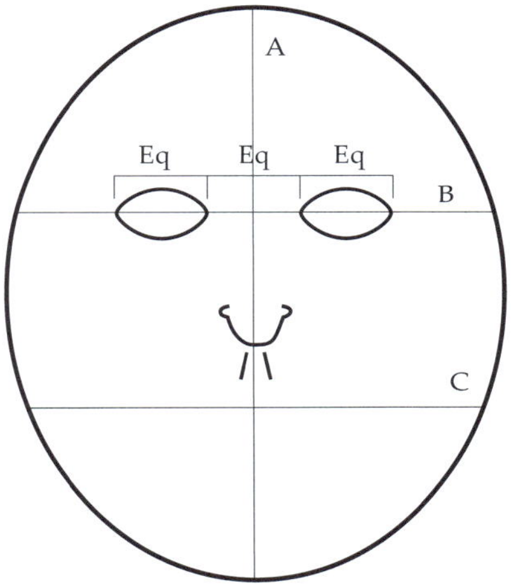

2. For the nose, have students draw a small "smile," or a soft V shape, 2/3 of the way down from the eye line. Next, have them draw a "C" on the left of the "V." Repeat this process using a backward "C" on the right side of the "V." (see diagram to the right). Have them draw two short parallel lines below the nose as shown in the diagram; this is the skin that connects the upper lip and the nose. Have students look at the person next to them so that they can visualize what they are drawing.

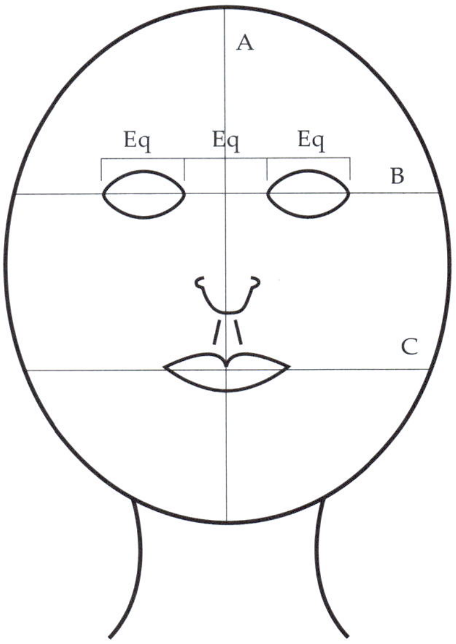

3. For the mouth, have them start on the intersection of line A and C. Starting at the center and drawing an arching line up and out, create the right side of the upper lip. Repeat the process for the other side. Some students call these frown faces, or upside-down smiles. Last, have them connect the outer edges with a "smile." (See diagram to the right.)
4. For the neck, students will add two lines. It is important to explain that the neck holds up the head, so it must be in proportion with the head. If the neck is too thin, the head would fall off because the neck would be unable to support the weight. Also, if the neck is too big, it will not look natural and the head will appear to have sunken into the body. See the diagram to the right for an example of proper proportions.
5. To finish up the portrait, have the students add in details like eyeballs and hair. This is an opportunity to allow them to use their own creativity.

Optional: Students may glue on yarn for hair to add a 3D-effect to their portraits.

PROJECT 4A: Line, Texture, and Color Portrait; Portrait of a Scarecrow

REVIEW

Line Types:

- *Continuous* — A solid line
- *Zigzag* — A combination of diagonal lines that connect at each point
- *Dotted or Dashed* — A line that is broken into segments or patterns
- *Curvy* — A line with soft bends and no angles

Textures:

- *Continuous* — A pattern or image created with smooth, uninterrupted lines (without picking up the pencil, pen, or brush to break the line at any point)
- *Stipple/Dot* — A pattern or image created with dots
- *Crosshatch* — Parallel lines that intersect each other, used to shade or mark an image
- *Blending/Gradation* — A gentle and gradual transition from dark to light

WEEK ONE

MATERIALS NEEDED

- ☐ 11″ x 17″ white card stock or paint-grade paper, two per student
- ☐ Paint: primary colors and brown
- ☐ Mixing tray
- ☐ Paintbrushes

INSTRUCTIONS

Have students paint 6″ squares of red, yellow, and blue on the 11″ x 17″ paper. Then have them mix secondary colors and repeat on the second piece of paper. Lastly, have the students paint one more additional square using brown.

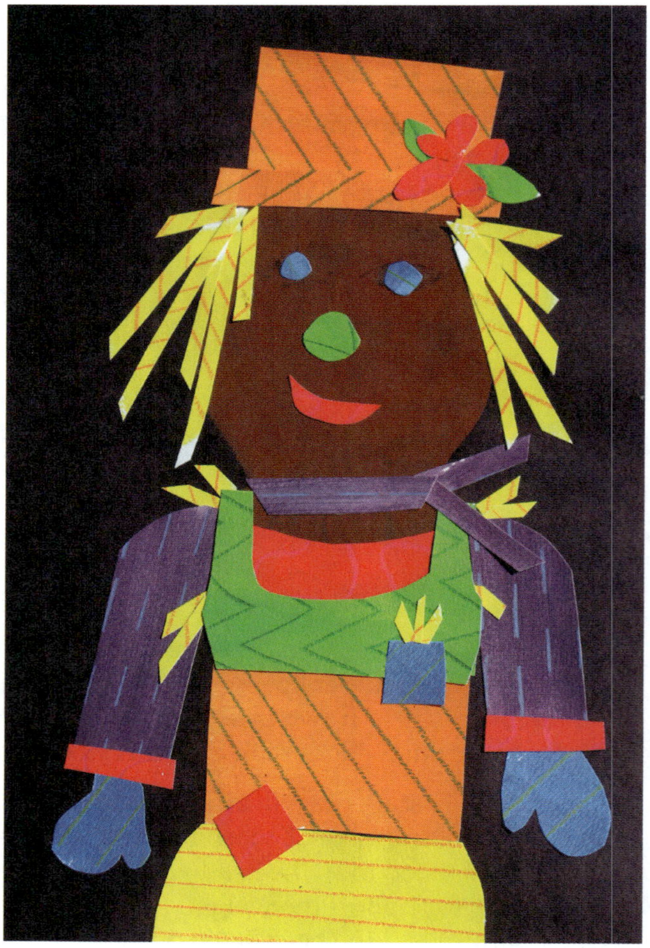

WEEK TWO

MATERIALS NEEDED

- ☐ 11″ x 17″ black paper, one per student
- ☐ Colored pencils
- ☐ Rulers
- ☐ Scissors
- ☐ Glue or glue stick
- ☐ Template of scarecrow head

INSTRUCTIONS

1. With a colored pencil in a contrasting hue to the painted square, have students draw different line types on top of each square. Next, in a collage format, have the students create a picture of a scarecrow's face using the painted squares, and following the proportion system for portraits.
2. When the students have finished the head portion, have them use the remaining paint squares to create a body for their scarecrow. This is a great time to allow the students creative freedom.

LESSON 5: Landscapes

REVIEW

Portrait Format — The format used for a portrait; a rectangle that is taller than it is wide

Oval — The space around the subject in a portrait to contain proper proportions. This is not always visible; it is often implied

Breathing Area — The space outside the oval

Textures:

» ***Continuous*** — A pattern or image created with smooth, uninterrupted lines (without picking up the pencil, pen, or brush to break the line at any point)

» ***Stipple/Dot*** — A pattern or image created with dots

» ***Crosshatch*** — Parallel lines that intersect each other, used to shade or mark an image

» ***Blending/Gradation*** — A gentle and gradual transition from dark to light

TERMS TO KNOW

Landscape Format — The format used for landscapes; a rectangle that is wider than it is tall

Landscape — A depiction of the outdoors

Horizon Line — A line that separates the land/water from the sky

GENERAL FACTS

1. **There are three parts to a landscape:**
   » ***Foreground*** — Objects that are close up and in the front; also referred to as the front ground (*usually flowers, bushes, and smaller things; more detailed and focused)*

   » ***Middle Ground*** — Usually the focal point of the landscape *(usually houses, animals, and people)*

   » ***Background*** — The far distance *(usually mountains and trees)*
2. **Framing** — When the foreground, usually a tree or a vine, rises up along the sides to "frame" the subject or focal point
3. **Depth** — Using objects to give a visual perception, which draws viewers into a picture, or draws their focus to a particular object

ACTIVITIES

This is a visual reminder of the three parts of a landscape:

Choose three students of different heights. Place them in the front of the classroom, single file, several feet apart. Standing by the shortest person, name them Foreground. The student in the middle is Middle Ground, and the student in the rear is Background. Have Foreground kneel, have Middle Ground sit in a chair, and have Background stand. Explain that Foreground is completely visible and the closest to the class, allowing viewers to see the details of their features. Middle Ground is somewhat blocked by Foreground, yet their face, which is the focal point, is completely visible, thus drawing attention to the main element. Background is not only the farthest away, but is blocked by both Foreground and Middle Ground, thus making them less noticeable.

CLASS	X **Foreground**	X **Middle Ground**	X **Background**	WALL

PROJECT 5: Landscapes

MATERIALS NEEDED

- ☐ 8.5″ x 11″ white paper
- ☐ Ruler
- ☐ Pencil
- ☐ Colored pencils

INSTRUCTIONS

1. Have students place a white piece of paper in the landscape position. Have students use the ruler to draw a horizontal line or a horizon line approximately 2/3 of the way up from the bottom of the page. Above the horizon line, students draw triangles to create a mountain region. They may layer the triangles to create depth by having them recede to the back or cross over each other to the left or right.

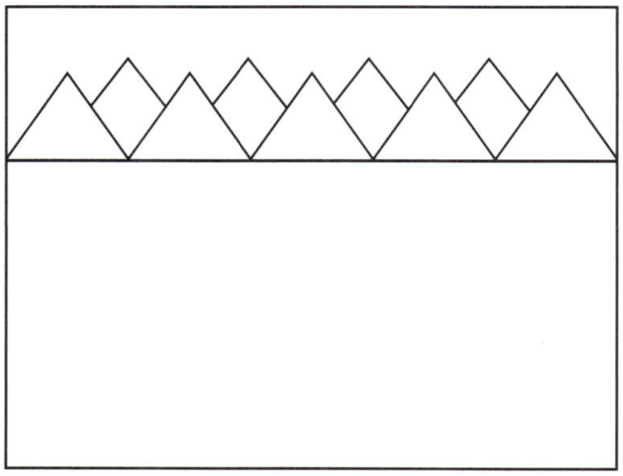

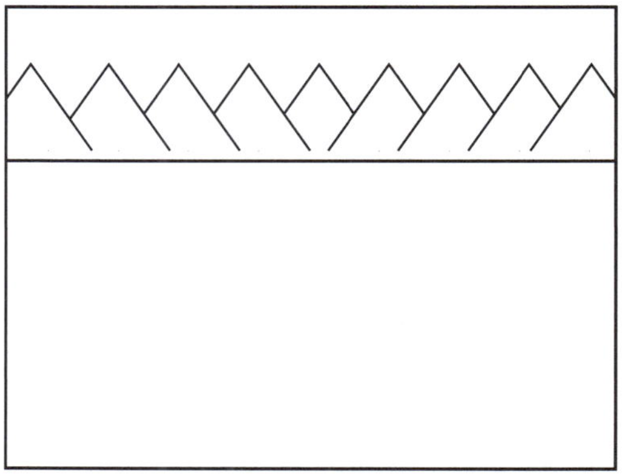

2. In the center of the page, below the horizon line, have students draw an animal or animals. Overlapping animals is a great way to show depth. Remember that the farther back the object is, the smaller it will appear. Also, the animals do not need to have a lot of intricate details. Good options are sheep, horses, and/or cows.
3. Next, have the students draw small bushes in the lower two corners. These can have flowers and various details, as they are meant to be up close with clear detail. (See example below.) If time permits, add a tree behind a bush that follows the edge of the paper and creates a frame or framing.

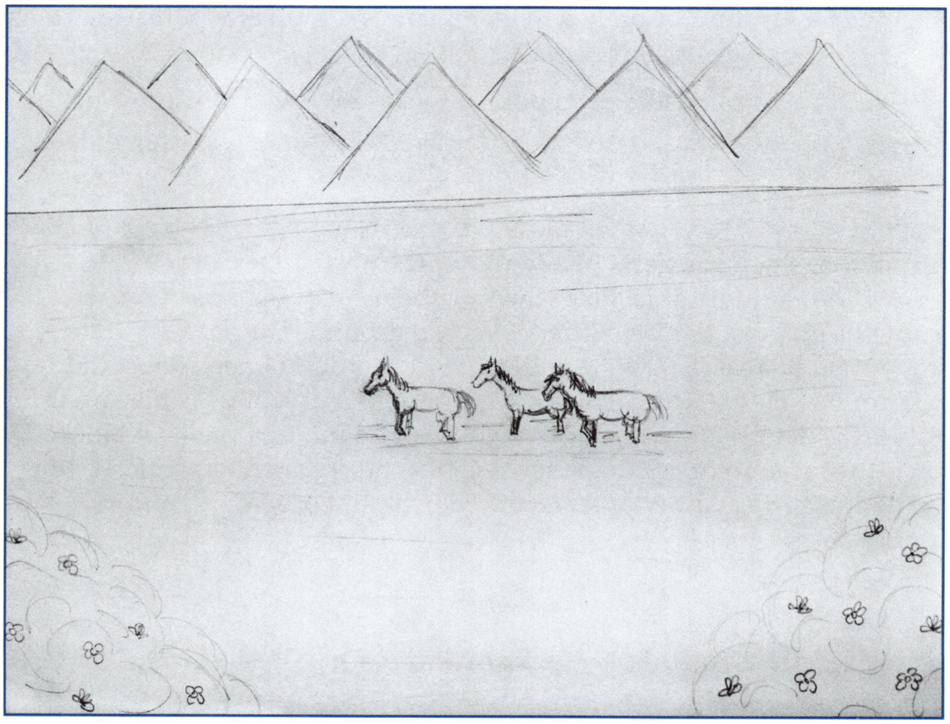

4. Last, have students color in the landscape.
   A. When using colored pencils, start by coloring the whole object or shape with a base color.
   B. Next, add a shade, or darker value of the base color, to create depth or shadow.
   C. Last, sharpen edges and add detail by using black.
   D. Remember: The farther back you go, the lighter or "foggier" the objects become.

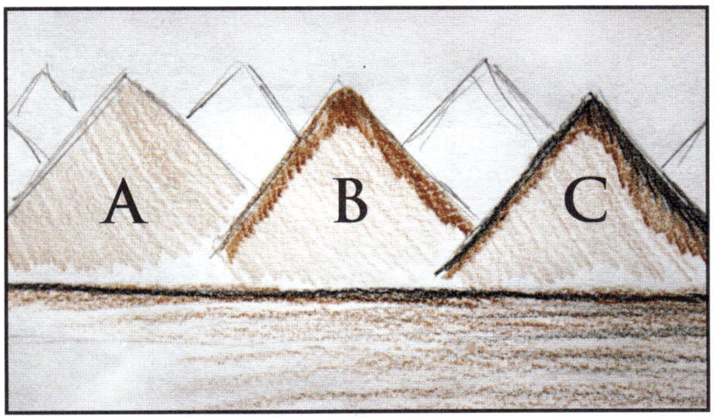

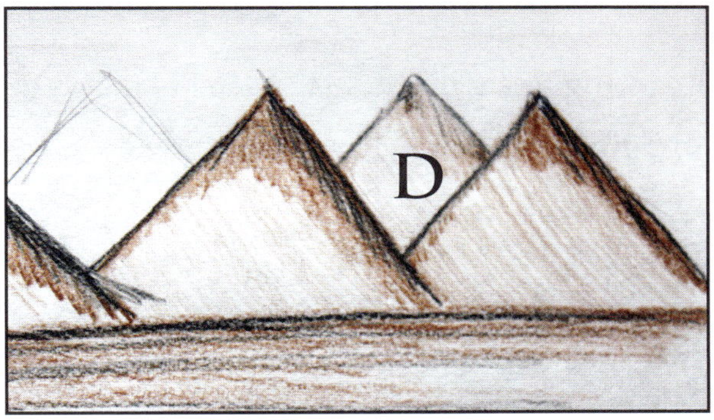

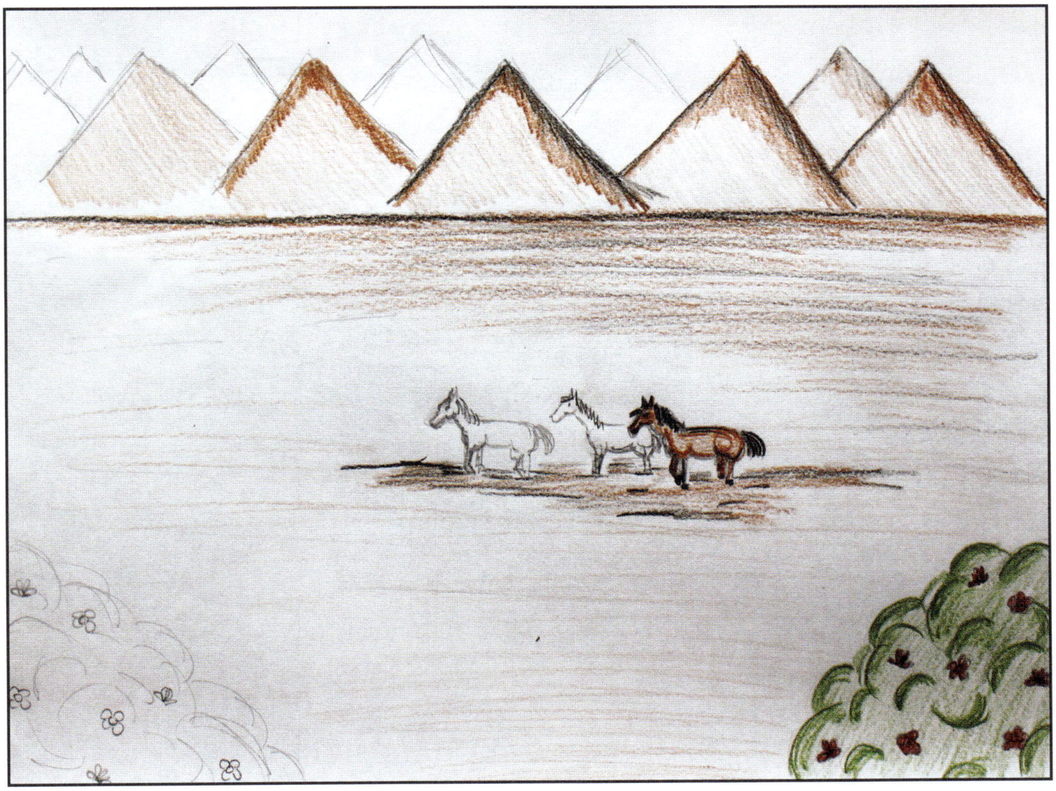

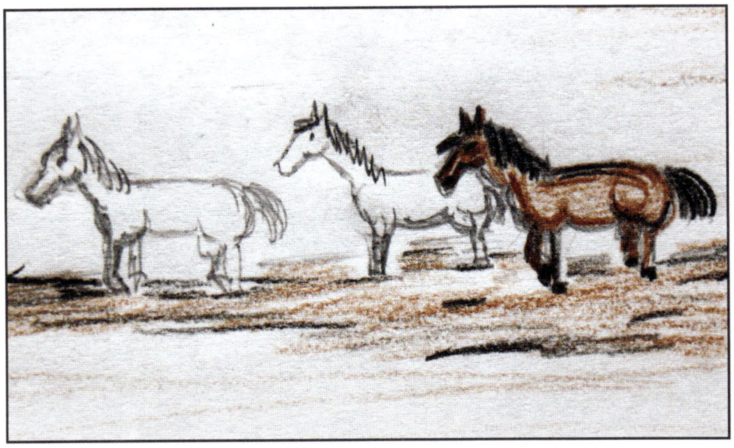

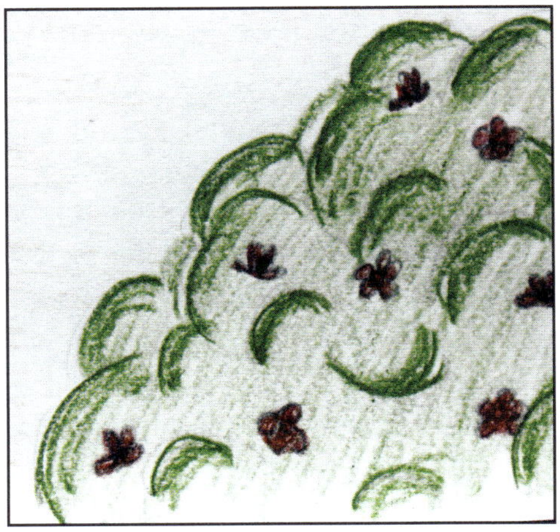

LESSON 6: Prehistoric Art – Cave Painting

REVIEW

Portrait Format — The format used for a portrait; a rectangle that is taller than it is wide

Oval — The space around the subject in a portrait to contain proper proportions. This is not always visible; it is often implied.

Breathing Area — The space outside the oval

Landscape Format — The format used for landscapes; a rectangle that is wider than it is tall

Landscape — A depiction of the outdoors

Horizon Line — A line that separates the land/water from the sky

TERMS TO KNOW

Prehistoric — Before written history

Pigment Powder — Colorful powder made from the dust of crushed minerals

Bone Tubes — Hollowed-out bones used to store pigment powder

GENERAL FACTS

1. Cave paintings are some of the earliest recorded art.
2. They are found all over the world: Europe, South America, Australia, and Africa.
3. The two most published caves are located in France: the Lascaux, and the Chauvet.
4. Each cave has different animals in it.
5. Many of these paintings are located in hard-to-reach places, and most locations give no evidence of habitation or dwelling.
6. **Chauvet Cave:** Rhinos, lions, bears, panthers, and owls
7. **Lascaux Cave:** Bison, horses, stags, bulls, aurochs, and mammoths (Aurochs are an extinct form of cattle.)
8. Why paint animals?
   - Religious reasons
   - To remember the animals' appearance – record keeping
   - Storytelling – historical documentation
   - Superstition – to ward off illnesses and evil spirits
9. How did the artists paint, and with what?
   - They used natural materials as tools:
     - » Hollowed-out sticks and bones
     - » Stripes or pads of leather
     - » Feathers
     - » Fur
     - » Sticks
     - » Fingers
     - » Hair
   - They made color or paint from minerals.
   - They crushed these minerals into a powder and put the powder onto a moist surface, which would cause the powder and water to mix and create a paste or paint-like substance similar to what we know today.
   - This powder is referred to as **pigment powder**.
   - Sometimes they mixed the powder with wax or oils so that it would stick to bone and leather.
   - They would store the pigment powder in hollowed-out bones called **bone tubes**.

10. Colors used and their sources:

- Black – charcoal or burned bones
- Violet – magnesium
- White – caulk, bone, or calcite
- Green/blue – special rock (rare and hard to find, possibly jade)
- Red – red ocher
- Yellow – yellow ocher

11. Where did the artists paint, and why?

- Cave walls
- Rocks
- Animal hides
- Wood
- Bone

Cave walls and large rocks were fixed and permanent locations, often protected from weather and other things that would cause them to deteriorate. Animal hides, wood, and bone were more portable and easily moved; thus if artists moved, they could take their art with them. Portable art may have been similar to a photo book, family album, or family history item. Several of the cave paintings are 15-18 feet long and 10-20 feet high. When we look at paintings today, we usually know who created them because artists often sign their work. When these cave paintings were drawn, written language was not yet invented; there were no letters to spell with. So how did others know who painted these amazing paintings? The artist left a signature, or identifying mark, by placing a hand near the painting and blowing pigment powder onto it from a bone tube, much like dipping a straw in colored chalk dust and blowing it out the other end. As the powder hit the moist surface of the cave, the water and powder mixed and created paint. When the hand was removed, its outline was left behind, and the painting was thus signed.

PROJECT 6: Prehistoric Art – Cave Drawing

MATERIALS NEEDED

- ☐ 8.5″ x 11″ butcher paper*
- ☐ Chalk in brown, black, white, red, and yellow
- ☐ Animal Templates (Pre-cut card stock)
- ☐ Hand Template (Pre-cut card stock)

*The inside of a paper grocery bag works well. Construction paper may tear if it is too thin. Card stock does not work.

INSTRUCTIONS

1. Give each student a piece of butcher paper and have them crumple it up into a ball and smooth it out three times. Be careful; the paper can tear if the students get too aggressive.
2. Each student should choose two animals they would like to use. Have them hold the first animal template on the paper and, using brown chalk, trace the animal with their opposite hand.
3. Repeat this with the second animal. Next, have the students use the other colors to add details to the animals; shade, shadows, and highlights. Make sure the students do not color in the animal completely. Pigment powder was not easy to make, so it would have been used sparingly.
4. Last, when the students have finished with the animals, have them hold the hand template in place and outline it. While holding the template in place, rub the black chalk away from, or out from, the hand.

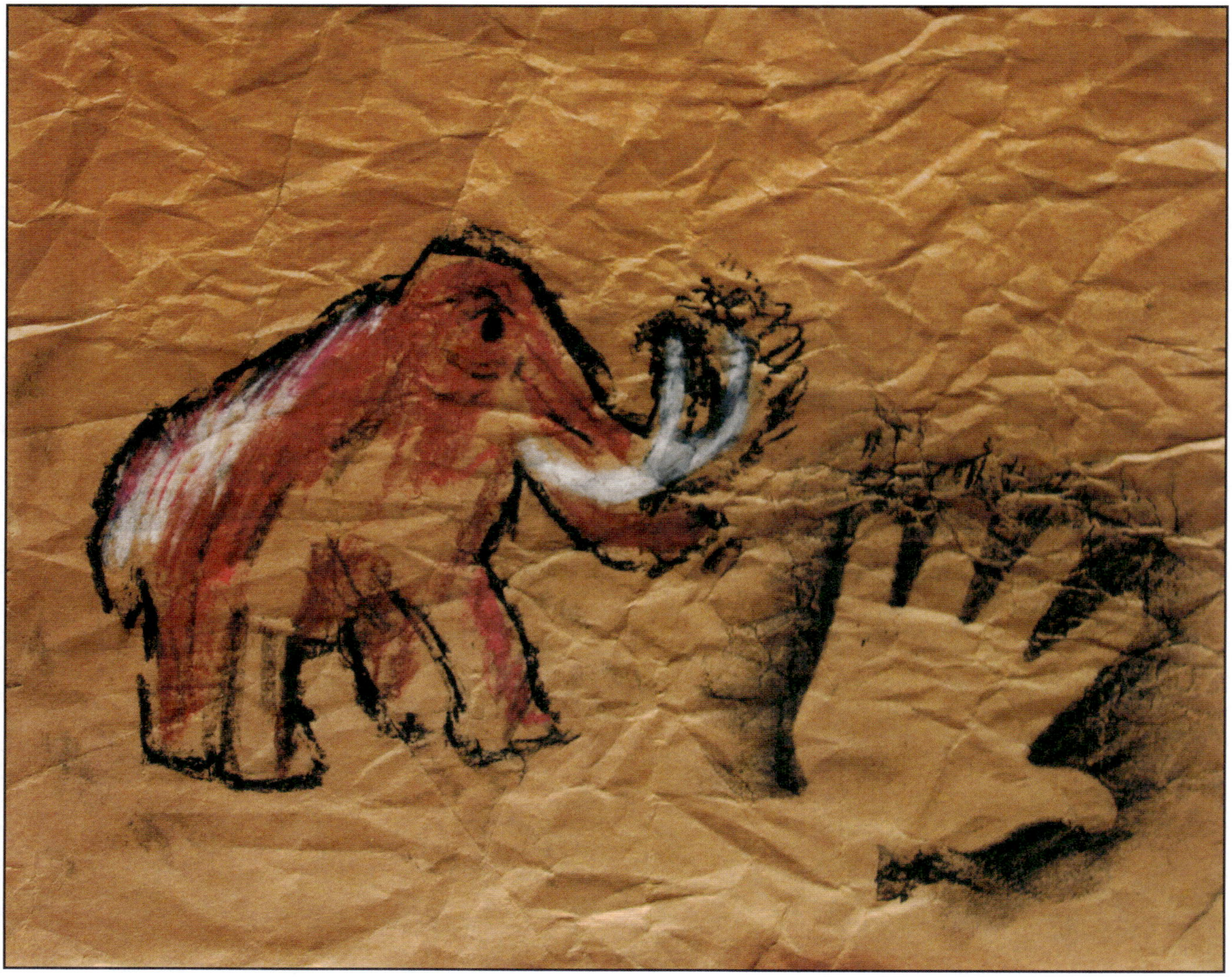

LESSON 7: Mesopotamian Art

REVIEW

Prehistoric — Before written history

Pigment Powder — Colorful powder made from the dust of crushed minerals

Bone Tubes — Hollowed-out bones used to store pigment powder

Colors used and their sources:

- » Black – charcoal or burned bones
- » Violet – magnesium
- » White – caulk, bone, or calcite
- » Green/blue – special rock (rare and hard to find, possibly jade)
- » Red – red ocher
- » Yellow – yellow ocher

TERMS TO KNOW

Mesopotamia — "Land between two rivers," i.e., the land between the Tigris and Euphrates Rivers

Sculpture in the Round — A multi-level group of statuettes that signify social standing

Standard — A banner or flag

Mosaic — A picture or design created with small stones or shells

GENERAL FACTS

1. **Mesopotamia** means "land between two rivers," that is, the Tigris and the Euphrates. The art from this time period depicts mostly mythical creatures. These mythical creatures were combinations of human parts and animal parts. For example, a centaur is a horse's lower body with a human upper body.
2. Sculpture was the most common form of art.
   - Most sculptures of this time period were done in clay, largely because of the materials available in the region.
3. A **sculpture in the round** is a multi-level group of statuettes that signify social standing. Statues in the sculpture are not arranged in a circle, as the title suggests; rather, they are arranged in rows by height, showing status, power, or authority. The taller the statue, the more power or authority it represents. The tallest statue represents a priest; the next statue would be a worshiper, and the smallest statues represent servants or persons of insignificance. The men have beards, and the detail of the beard indicates the amount of power each man has within his social status group. The more ornamental and detailed the beard, the more power and authority; the simplest beard represented a common person.

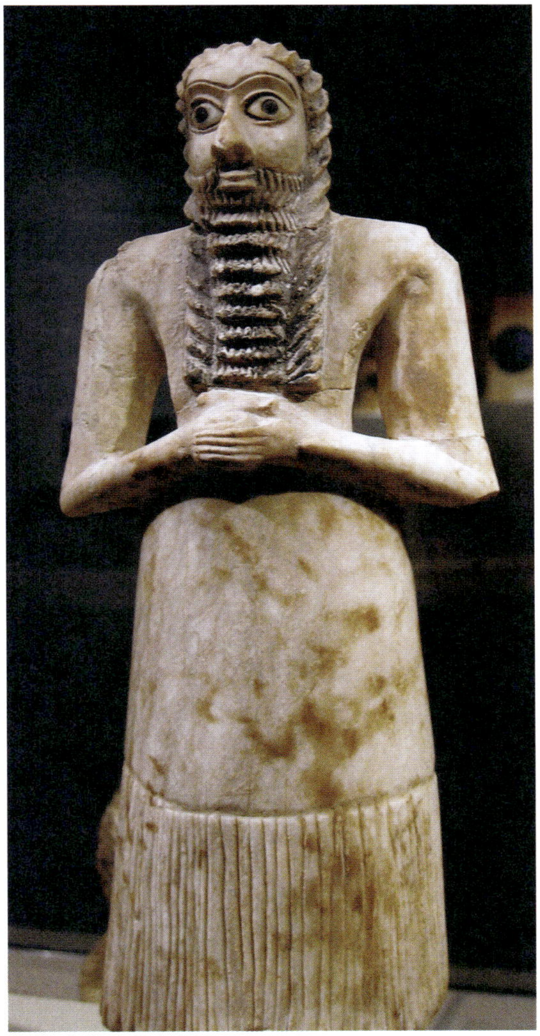

Sculpture in the round: *Standing male worshiper*

Mesopotamia, Iraq - Sumerian Figure by Xuan Che (https://flic.kr/p/8EB3s)

4. A **cylinder seal** is a small cylinder-shaped stone that is carved with symbols. These stones were carved with unique markings that referred to a particular business, family, group, or ritual. The cylinders were rolled across soft clay to create a plate or plaque. Some uses for cylinder seals:
    - To decorate doors or gates
    - For use in rituals
    - To mark ships or vessels
    - Amulets
    - To tag or identify personal property
    - To show authority

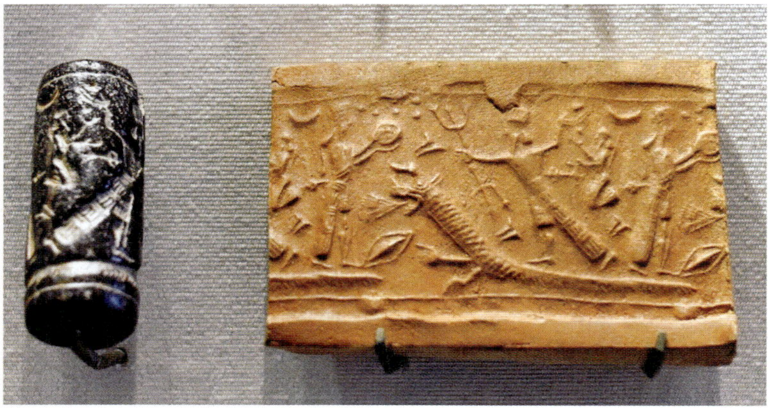

Cylinder seal and clay imprint

5. A **ziggurat** was an ancient building made in a pyramid-type shape. The ziggurat was considered a temple or place of worship where Heaven and Earth were linked.

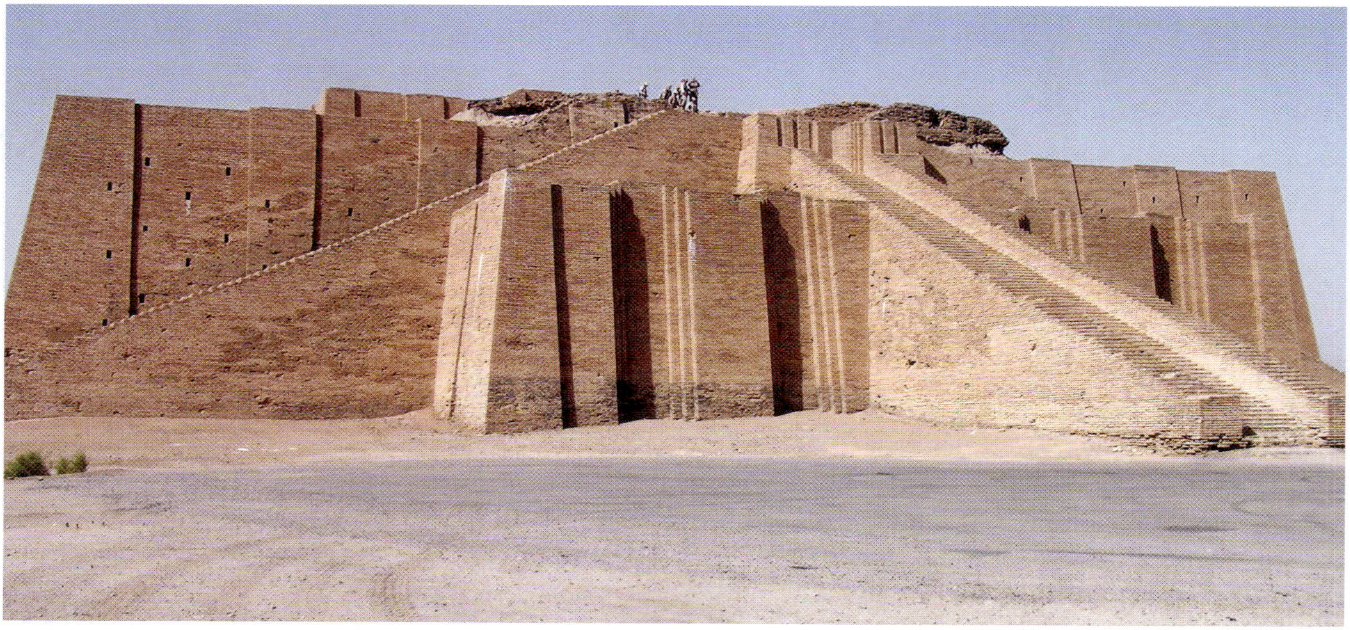

Ancient Ziggurat at Ali Air Base, Iraq

Photo by Hardnfast (http://bit.ly/1eZrQrJ) | License: CC BY 3.0 (https://creativecommons.org/licenses/by/3.0/deed.en)

6. The word **standard** literally means "banner" or "flag." Ancient banners contain scenes that tell a story through a series of panels, sort of like a modern-day newspaper comic strip. The most famous standard is the Standard of Ur. One side tells of peace and the other of war.

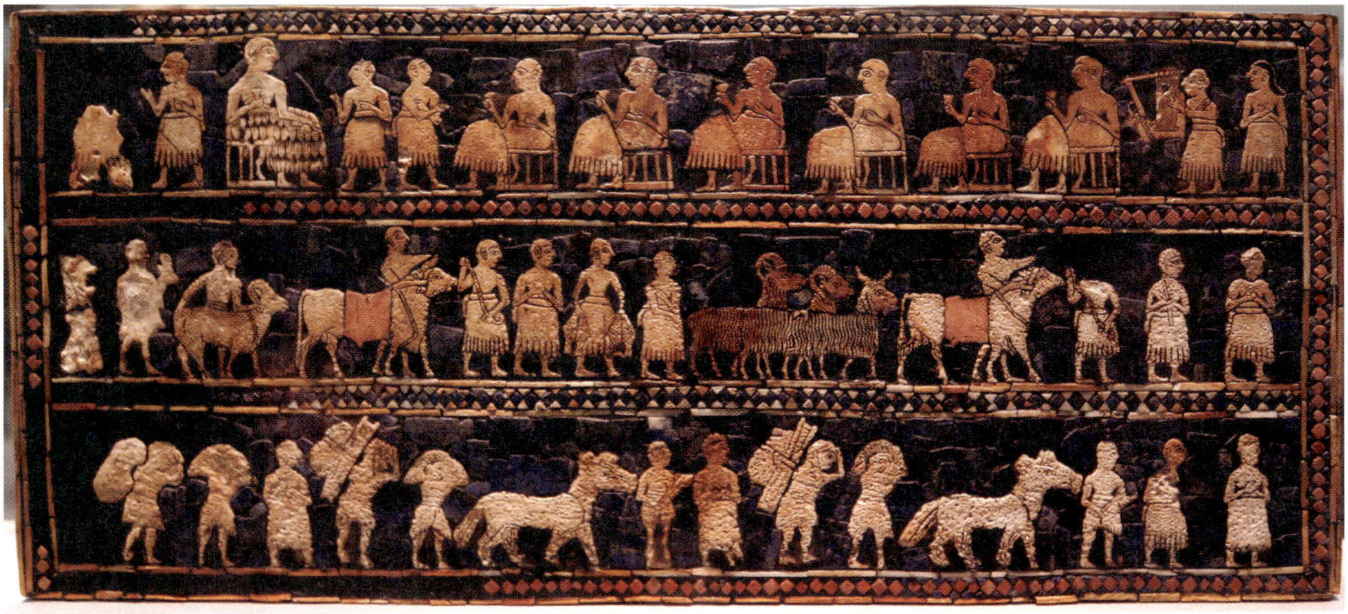

Peace Panel of the Standard of Ur

Photo by Geni (http://bit.ly/1Htp6dJ) | License: CC BY SA 3.0 (https://creativecommons.org/licenses/by-sa/3.0/deed.en)

7. A **mosaic** is a picture or design created with small stones or shells. Mosaics come in many different sizes and are created for many reasons. Some were made in a small form as decoration; some covered entire walls or floors. Mosaics can be used as symbols or they can tell a story.

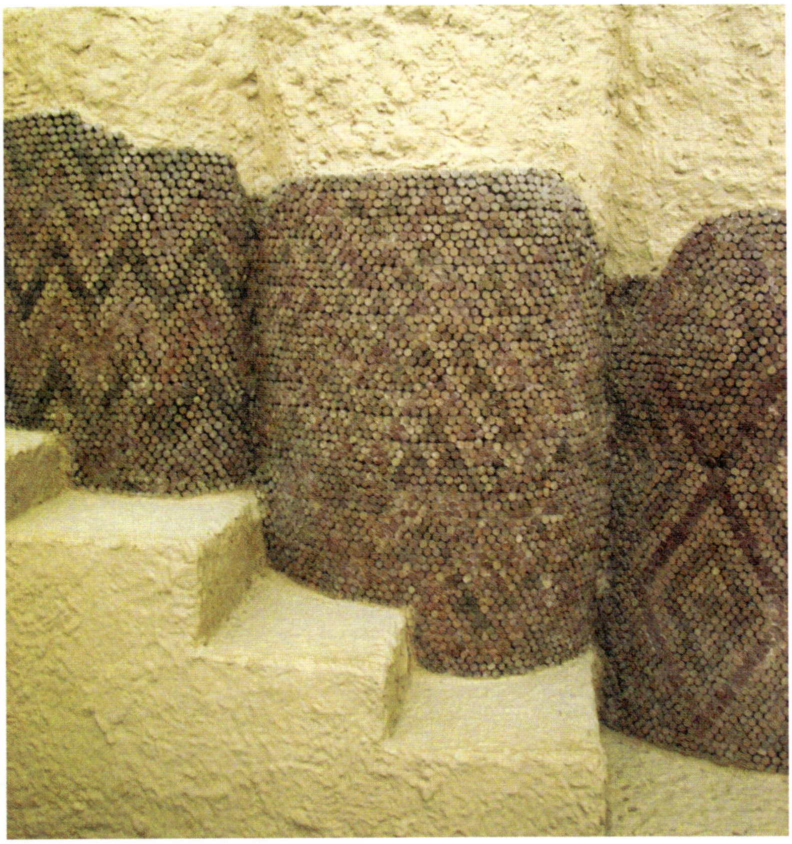

Cone mosaic courtyard from Uruk, in Mesopotamia, 3000 B.C.

Photo by Hahaha (http://bit.ly/1M87GKi) | License: CC BY SA 2.5 (https://creativecommons.org/licenses/by-sa/2.5/deed.en)

PROJECT 7: Mesopotamian Art – Mosaics

(This is a two-week project.)

MATERIALS NEEDED

- ☐ Pre-dyed Ditalini noodles (see instructions below). Colors include red, orange, yellow, green, blue, and purple.*
- ☐ Paper plates
- ☐ Craft glue
- ☐ Pencils
- ☐ Paintbrushes
- ☐ Small cups and bowls
- ☐ Sample Animal Templates

*Other shapes, such as stars, may also be used.

INSTRUCTIONS FOR DYED NOODLES *(Do this a day or two before the project.)*

1. In a gallon-size Ziplock bag, add enough noodles so that you can lay the bag flat, and add enough rubbing alcohol to cover the noodles.
2. Next, add food coloring; the more you add, the brighter the colors will be.
3. Lay the bags flat for a minimum of 30 minutes, then flip them over for another 30 minutes. (You may let the noodles steep longer; the longer they sit, the more saturated the color will be.)
4. When the desired color is obtained, spread the noodles on a cookie sheet lined with paper towels and allow them to dry. Once the noodles are dry, you are ready to start the project.

INSTRUCTIONS FOR MOSAICS

1. Start by having the students draw a picture of an animal or animal face on the plate. You may want to provide a few examples of simple animals; for example, fish, pig, frog, dog, etc. (see templates). Have students keep in mind the size of the noodle so that they do not make shapes that are tiny.
2. Next, have the students choose one noodle color to use at a time and put the noodles in a cup. Have students use the paintbrush to fill in small sections of their drawing with glue. (If they cover the whole plate with glue, it will dry before they are able to finish adding the noodles.) Make sure the students use a generous amount of glue or the noodles will fall off easily.
3. Make sure the students change noodle colors for different elements within their picture. (See example.) If time permits, you may allow them to fill in the background with one color that **contrasts** the **key** color of the design.

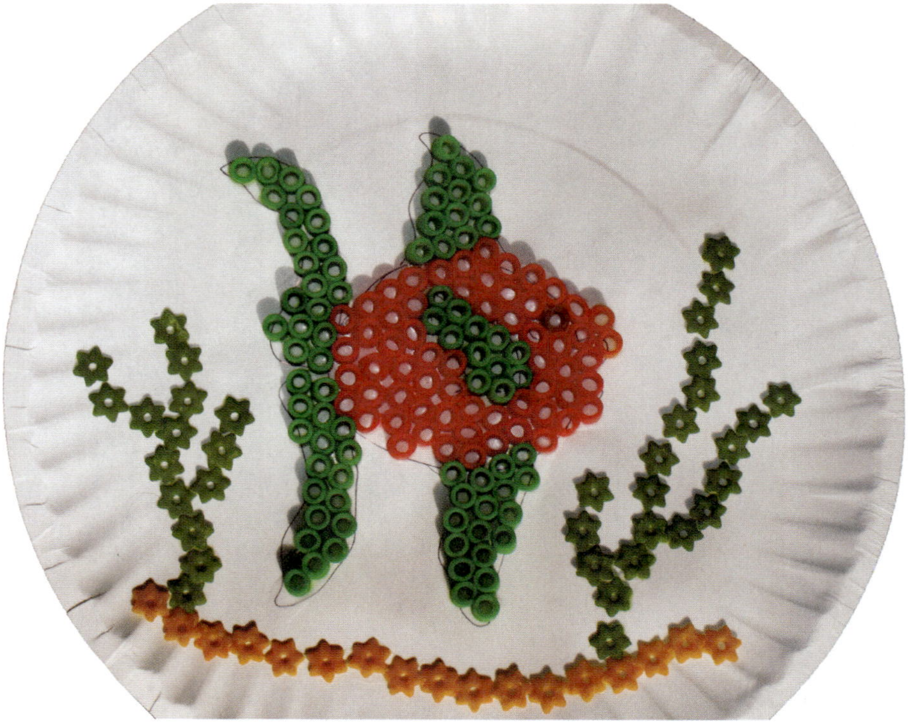

SPECIAL PROJECT 2: Valentine's Day Hearts

MATERIALS NEEDED

- ☐ 8.5″ x 11″ white paper
- ☐ 4 colored pencils of choice
- ☐ Optional: Various sized heart templates

INSTRUCTIONS

1. In the center of the paper, have the students draw one large heart and color it in. Next, draw a second heart slightly behind the first in a different color, and color it in. Repeat this process two more times with smaller hearts. Remember to keep all the hearts connected to at least one other heart. Next, have the students outline just the outer edge of the entire composition with one color. Continue to follow this process, switching colors each time and moving farther out, until the entire page is filled.

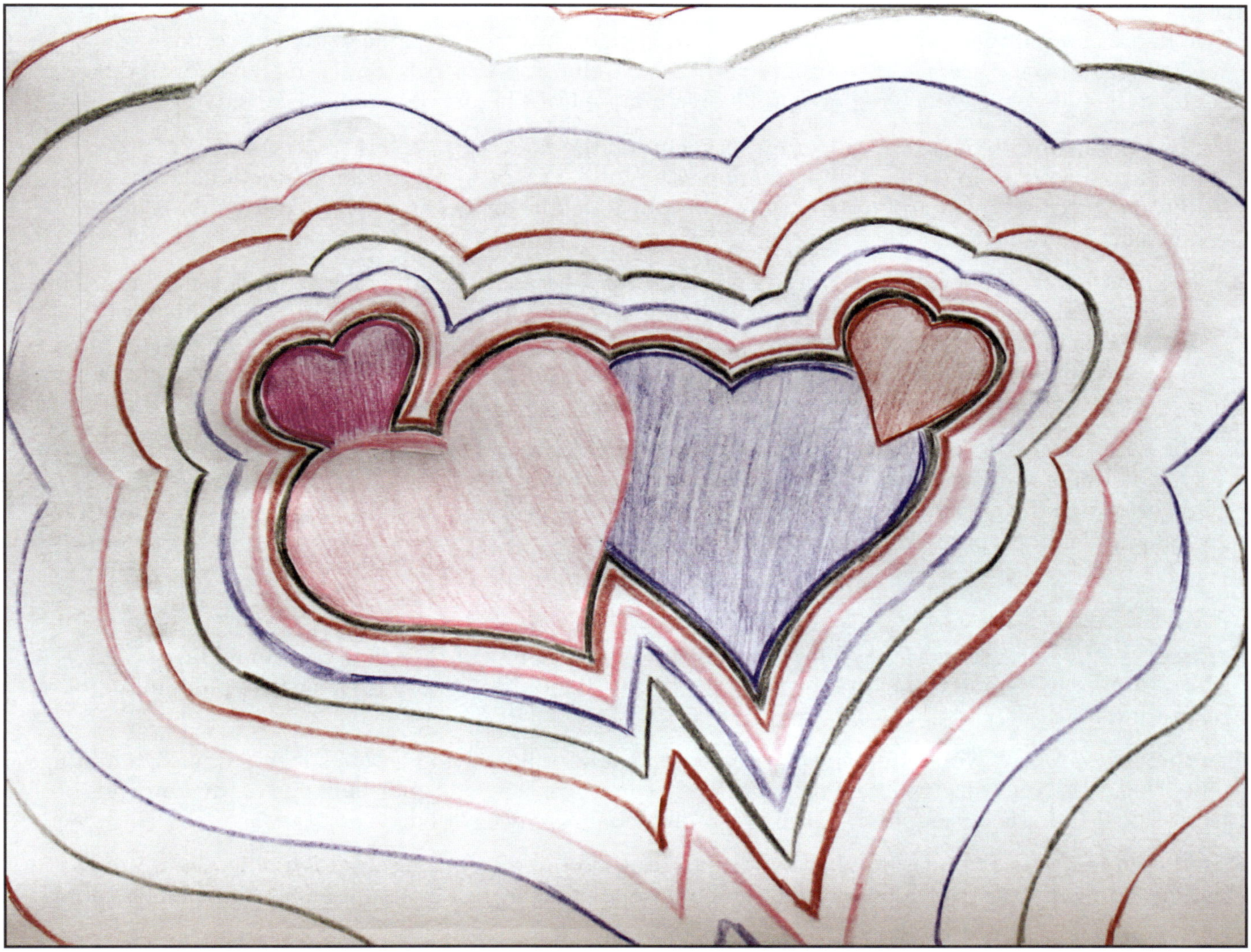

LESSON 8: Egyptian Art

REVIEW

Mesopotamia — "Land between two rivers," i.e., the land between the Tigris and Euphrates Rivers

Sculpture in the Round — A multi-level group of statuettes that signify social standing

Standard — A banner or flag

Mosaic — A picture or design created with small stones or shells

TERMS TO KNOW

Symbols of Lower Egypt — Red crown, cobra, and papyrus plant

Symbols of Upper Egypt — White crown, vulture, and lotus flower

Cartouche — An oval plaque that contains the name of an Egyptian god or royal

Rosetta Stone — A basalt slab that aided in the translation of hieroglyphics

Pectoral — A large ornate necklace worn over the chest, or pectoral muscles

GENERAL FACTS

1. Egyptian art reflects both the country's political position and its geographical position, so it is important to know about its geography and history to understand how the art came to be. The country was established from a union of Lower Egypt, the Nile Delta, and Upper Egypt, a small narrow strip of land along the Nile Valley. Each region had its own unique traits before the union occurred.

   Prior to the union, the art of Lower Egypt included the red crown, cobra snakes, and depictions of the papyrus plant. In Upper Egypt, there was a white crown, a vulture, and depictions of the lotus flower. Once the lower and upper regions became one, the art began to blend the symbols to form new compositions.

2. The Egyptian language does not have a word for "art" because they did not see these pieces as art, but as functional and necessary items for daily living. The Egyptians lived their entire lives preparing for death, so many of their art pieces are referred to as funeral art, i.e., items that would help them make their transition into the afterlife. The art was made with simple features so that it did not distract from the worship or task at hand. Figures in paintings and reliefs are in the **profile view**.

3. The Egyptians were known for outstanding low relief carving. Human figures were shown in the **profile view** with the head and feet, but the body was in a **full-face** view. Kings and gods were taller and towered over those below them to show authority and power. The backgrounds were kept simple and contained hieroglyphics to explain the picture.

TYPES OF ART

Register — A register shows a sequence of events in a cartoon-like fashion on a horizontal line-based pattern, similar to a standard. However, it differs from a standard in that it uses hieroglyphics in the background to explain the pictures.

Canopic Jar — A clay, wood, or stone jar used to store and protect the liver, intestines, stomach, and lungs as the dead pass from this life to the next. Each jar represents a specific guardian, one of the four sons of Horus. The lids of the jars are in the form of a human, baboon, dog, or falcon.

Rosetta Stone — A slab of basalt with identical writings in three languages: hieroglyphic, Greek, and Demotic, an Egyptian script used by priests. The Rosetta Stone is the key to understanding hieroglyphics.

Scarab — A large desert beetle and a symbol of great power in Egyptian mythology. Often carved in reliefs, jewelry, or as a small statuette.

Hieroglyphics — An ancient Egyptian language. The word literally means "sacred carving." Hieroglyphics is a system of pictures that represent objects and sounds.

Cartouche — An oval plate that contains the name of an Egyptian god or royal. This is an oval stone that has hieroglyphics of a particular name carved in a vertical pattern down the center. Around the edge of the stone is the loop rope, which is believed to have the power to protect the person named on the stone. The loop rope is a carved rope or a rope-like pattern.

SYMBOLS OF EGYPTIAN ART

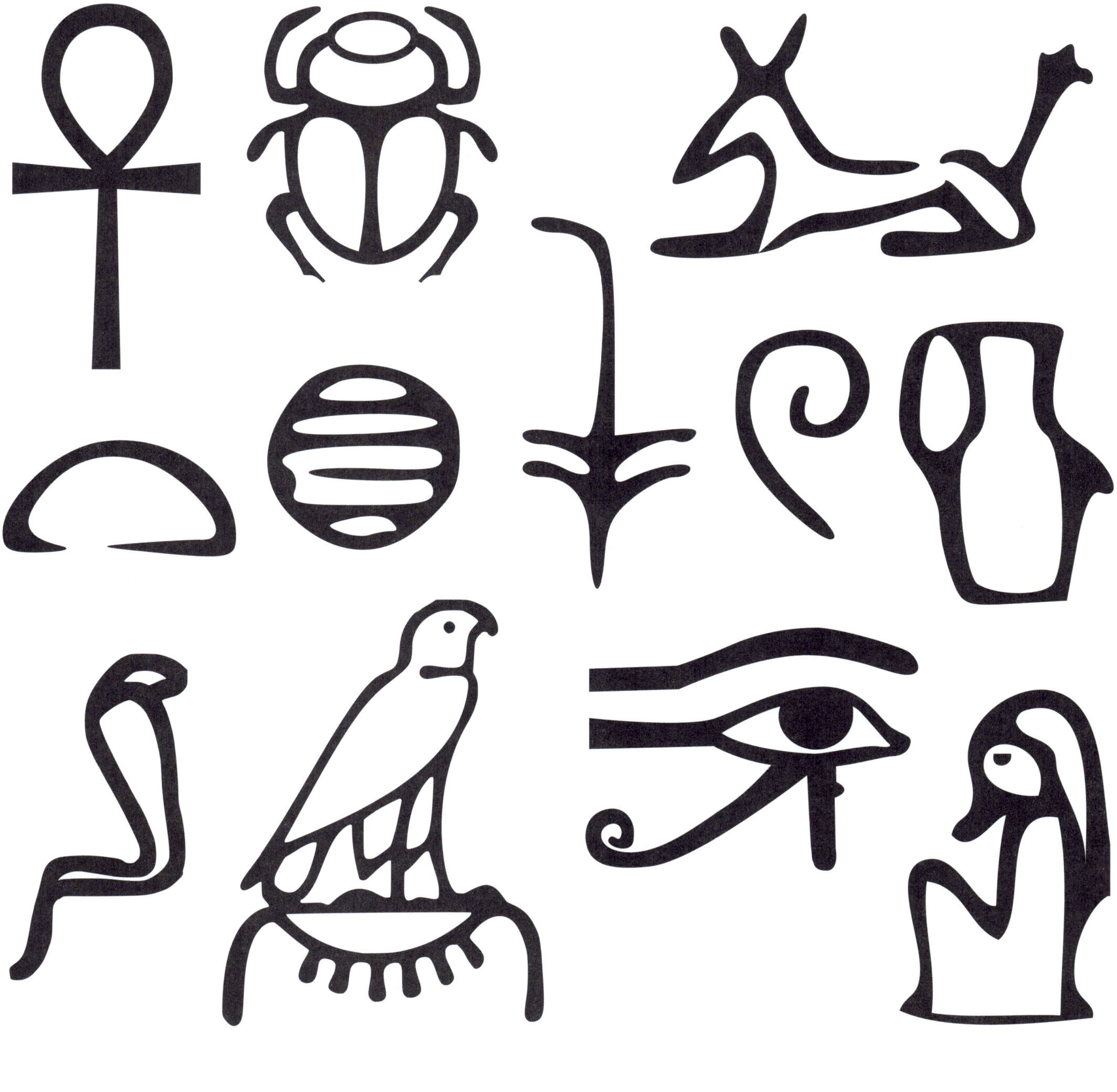

PROJECT 8: Egyptian Art – Pectorals

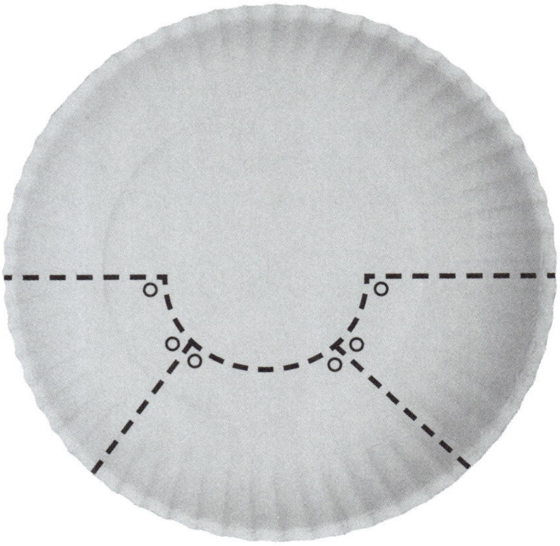

MATERIALS NEEDED

- ☐ Pre-cut and pre-punched paper plate
- ☐ Hole puncher
- ☐ Scissors
- ☐ Markers
- ☐ Yarn

INSTRUCTIONS

1. Have the students place the three plate pieces wax side down, or curved side down with the largest piece in the middle. Then have the students choose one set of complementary colors (or two colors that contrast) and create a stripe pattern along the curved bottom area of each piece.
2. Next, have students choose three symbols from Egyptian art to decorate the pieces in a symmetrical way. It is best to place one symbol in the center of the largest plate, then mirror the others on the left and on the right. Draw jewels and gems for a more ornate end product. The two small pieces will go on either side of the large piece and be connected by a long piece of yarn, which will create a band that will go around their neck.

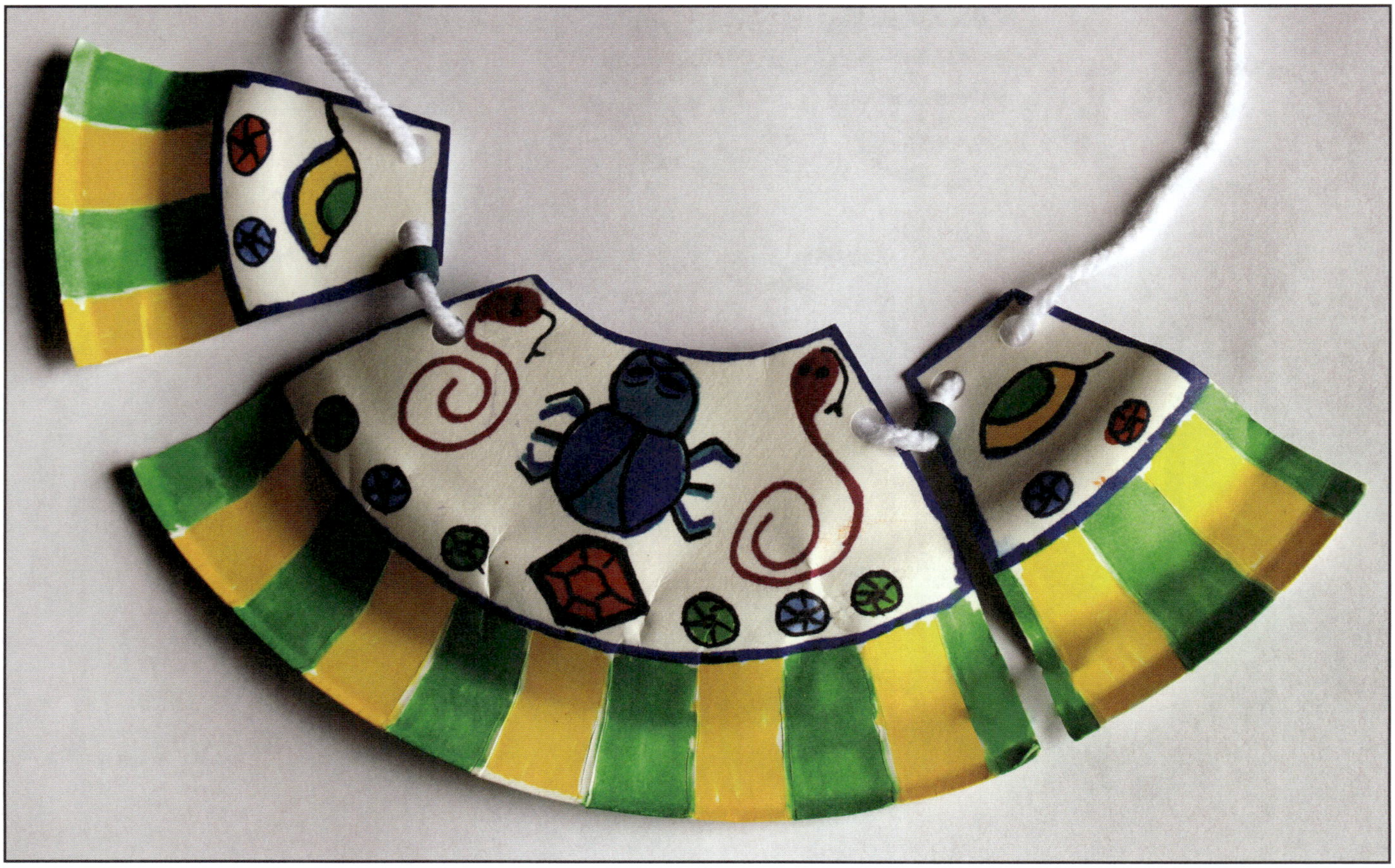

PROJECT 9: *Charlotte's Web* Wax Relief

MATERIALS NEEDED

- ☐ White watercolor paper
- ☐ Scratch paper
- ☐ Pencils
- ☐ Ruler
- ☐ White crayons (you can also use light yellow as shown in the upper left corner of the example)
- ☐ Watercolor paints
- ☐ Paintbrush

INSTRUCTIONS

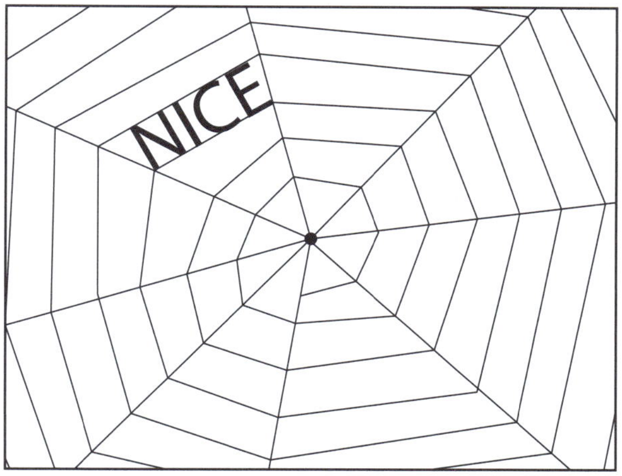

1. Talk with the students about the book *Charlotte's Web*. Refer to what Charlotte does to save Wilbur's life: she creates a web with words that describe her friend Wilbur.
2. Next, have the students think about some encouraging words that describe their friends (nice, fun, friendly, kind, etc.). Have scratch paper and pencils ready for them to write down their word in capital letters approximately 1″ high (using the ruler width as their guide) somewhere on the page. Set aside for reference.
3. Then, on the white watercolor paper, have students draw a dot somewhere on the page. Next, using the ruler, have them draw eight lines, arraying from the center to the outer edge of the paper. Have students rewrite their word on an angle between the arrayed lines. Then have them start at the center and create a spiral line that radiates out and connects to the letters of their word. Remind students that the connecting lines are to be straight, not curved.

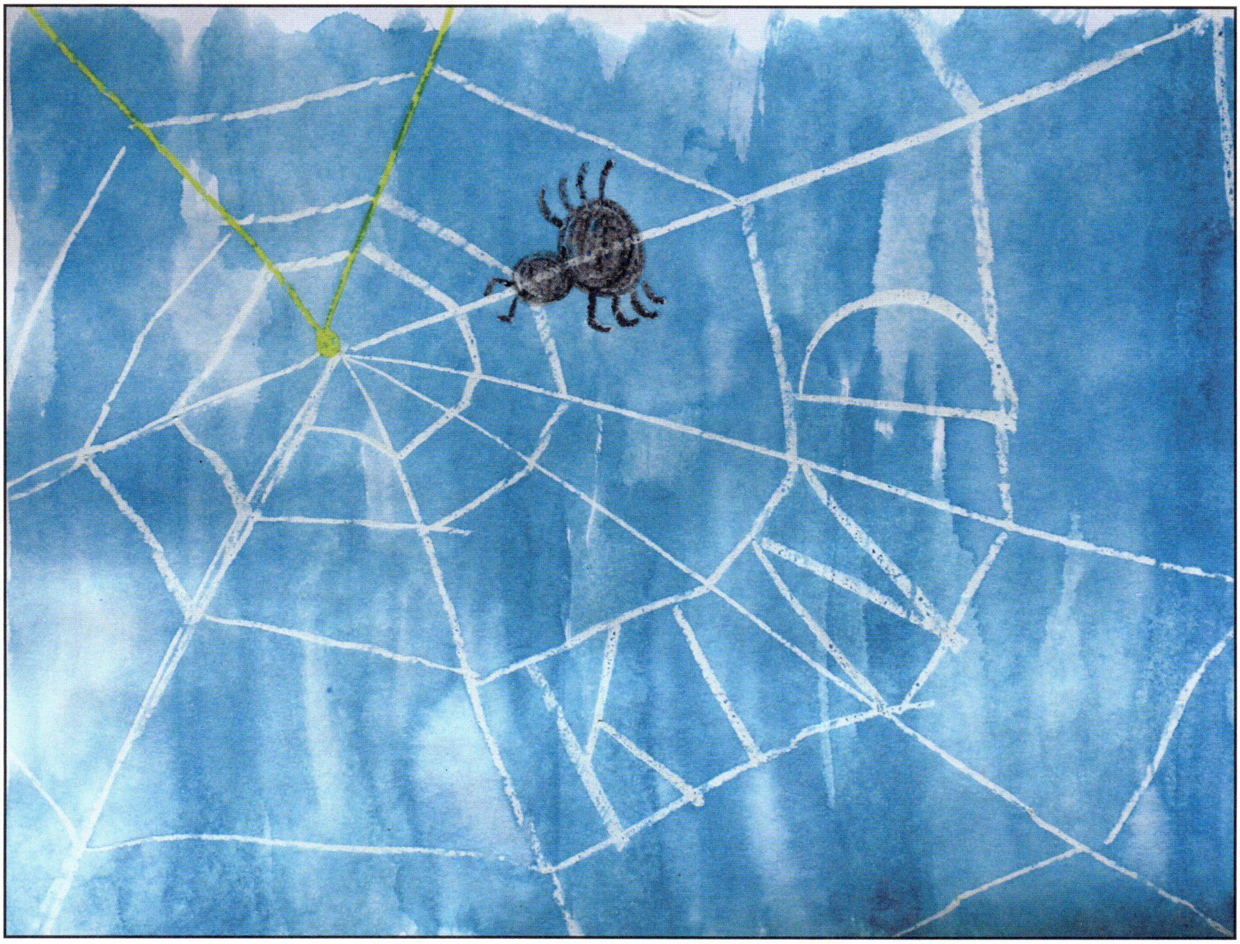

PROJECT 10: Astronomy – Glowing Constellations

MATERIALS NEEDED

- ☐ 11″ x 17″ black paper
- ☐ White and black paint
- ☐ Glow-in-the-dark paint
- ☐ Pencils
- ☐ Scratch paper
- ☐ Toothpicks

INSTRUCTIONS

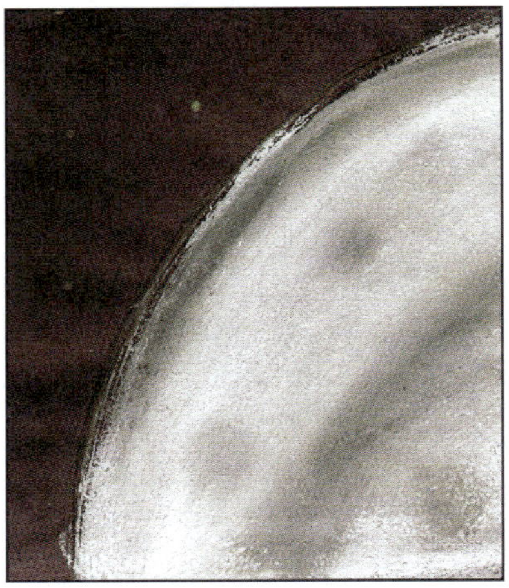

1. Have students write their name in all uppercase letters on a scratch piece of paper and set aside.
2. Using their fingers and white paint, have the students paint the moon in the lower right corner of the black paper.
3. Next, using a very small amount of black paint, have the students gently add some shadows by mixing the black paint into some of the white paint on the moon surface. Remind the students that the outer edge of the moon should maintain a white outline or edge.
4. Next, using the same finger, have students dab their finger on the wet painted surface of the moon and give a small twist. This will allow them to create a crater. I would limit the number of craters to three.

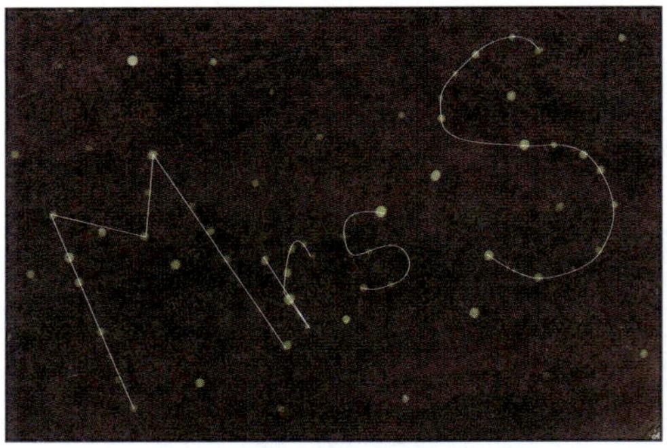

5. Next, have the students use the pencil to lightly dot out their name in the remaining space sky. Then have the students use the toothpick to dot over the pencil dots with glow paint. Make sure that they leave space between the dots so the name is not completely obvious.
6. After the paint has had a few minutes to dry, and the name has been completed, have the students use toothpicks and white paint to fill the space sky with other star dots.
7. You may want to add a few comets as well. This is done by making a larger dot for a star and then dragging the toothpick from the center of the dot out to the side.

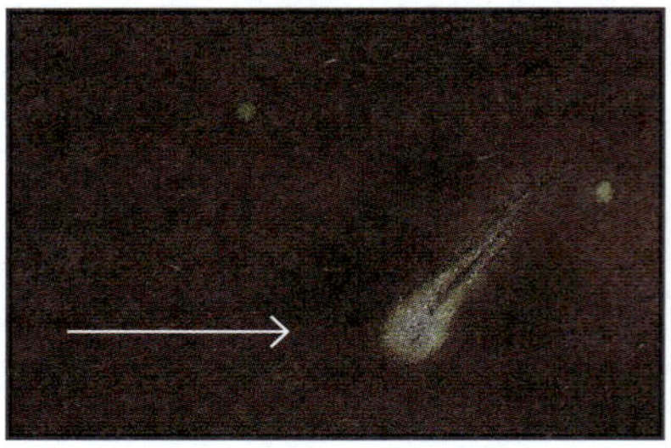

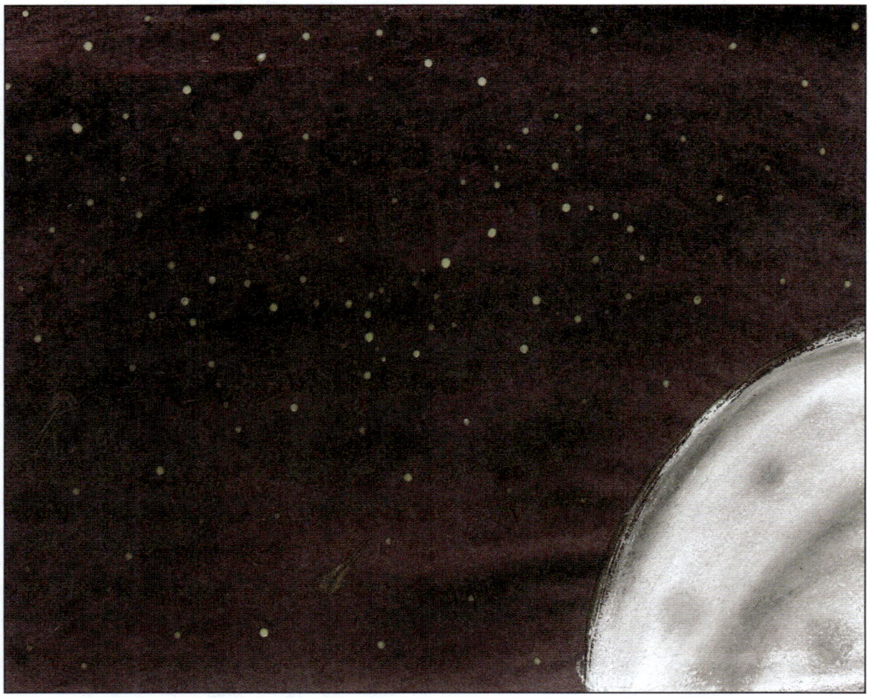

8. Once all the paint has dried and the paint has been exposed to light, have the students hold their paintings and turn off the lights. Their name should be the only thing that appears.

PROJECT 11: *The Moffats* – The Yellow House

MATERIALS NEEDED

- ☐ Construction paper (yellow, black, orange, blue, pink, green)
- ☐ Glue stick
- ☐ Scissors
- ☐ Ruler

INSTRUCTIONS

1. Have the students cut the blue construction paper into a rectangle approximately 6″x 8″.
2. Next, have the students glue the blue rectangle in the center of the yellow construction paper about 1″ from the top.
3. Then have the students cut thin black strips to outline the blue rectangle. Using two additional strips, create a cross-patterned mullion through the window.
4. Using the brown paper, have the students cut a rectangle that is 7″ long by 3″ tall. Fold the brown rectangle in half, left to right, and cut a small triangle off the 3″ end opposite the crease. (See diagram below.)

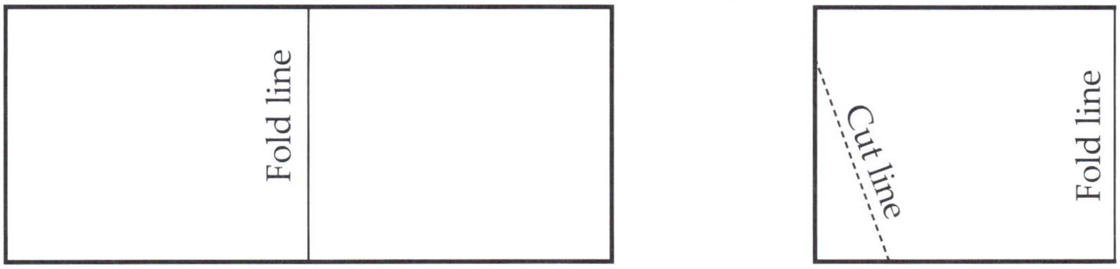

5. Next, unfold the brown rectangle and glue at the bottom of the window to create a flower box, leaving the top edge open (without glue). Have the students use the green construction paper to create stems and leaves for flowers. They will glue the stems at the top edge of the brown rectangle, so that they look like they have grown out of the box.
6. Last, using the orange and pink (or whatever colors you would like to provide) paper, have the students create their own types of flowers. I would recommend no more than 3-4 flowers.

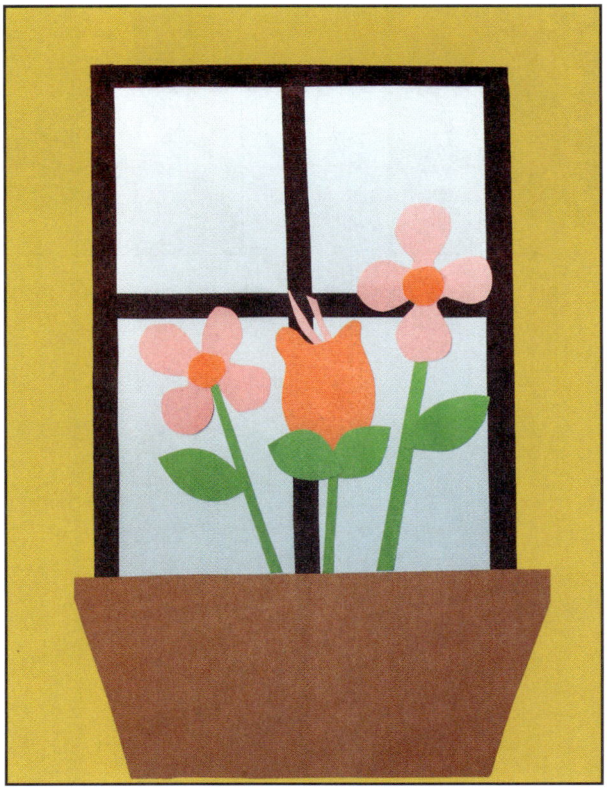

SPECIAL PROJECT 3: Decoupage Easter Eggs

MATERIALS NEEDED

- ☐ Multicolor tissue paper
- ☐ Paintbrushes
- ☐ Decoupage glue
- ☐ Papier-mâché or Styrofoam Easter eggs (Styrofoam shown in example)
- ☐ Wooden skewers
- ☐ Optional: straight pin and ribbon

INSTRUCTIONS

1. This is a really simple and fun project. Insert the skewer into the bottom of the egg. Have students tear small pieces of tissue paper. Next, have them brush the papier-mâché egg with decoupage glue. Using one small piece of tissue paper at a time, place it over the papier-mâché egg and brush with decoupage glue, covering the tissue paper completely. Continue this process until the whole egg is covered. Place the eggs on their skewers in a glass jar and allow the egg to dry.
2. If time and resources permit, allow students to make more than one.
3. **Optional:** Use a straight pin and glue to attach a ribbon to the top of the egg to create a hanging ornament instead of using the skewer.

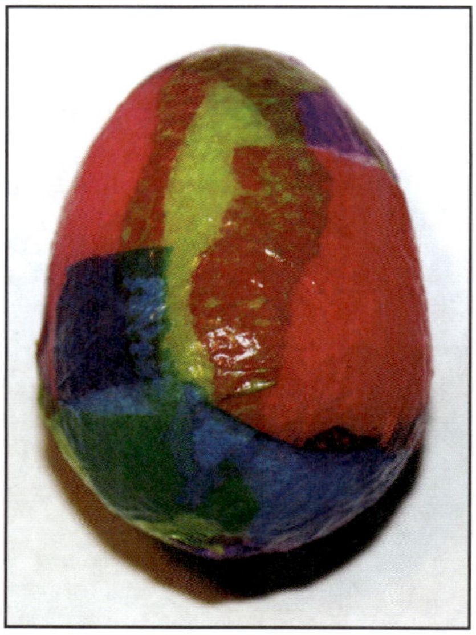

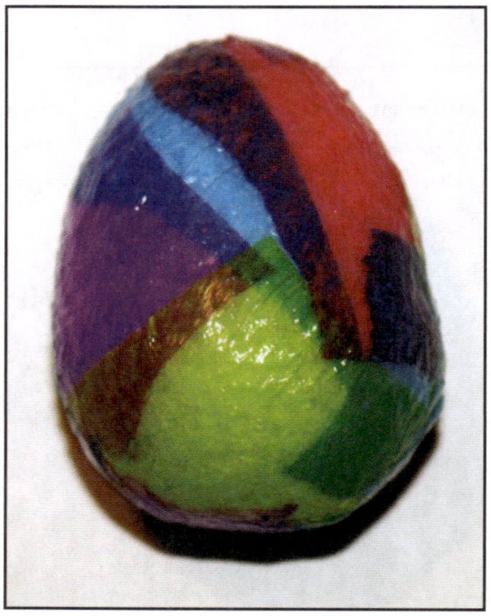

PROJECT 12: Still Life Vase Study – Pencil Drawing

TERMS TO KNOW

Still Life — A prearranged group of inanimate objects with contrasting textures; usually includes fruits, flowers, glass, or ceramics.

MATERIALS NEEDED

- ☐ Pencil
- ☐ Paper
- ☐ Vase
- ☐ Piece of plastic fruit

INSTRUCTIONS

1. Place a vase and a piece of fruit in a central location so that students can see it clearly. Have students use a pencil to draw what they see onto the piece of paper. This is a great time to help the students understand proportions. For instance, is the fruit the same size as the vase? If not, and if the vase is larger, explain that the fruit is a fraction of the height of the vase. It is good to have the students use the principles they learned when drawing portraits, such as guidelines—light lines that can easily be erased.
2. Have the students determine the light source by determining which way the shadows are cast. Also, remind students how to blend or gradate as they shade to allow for a more three-dimensional look.

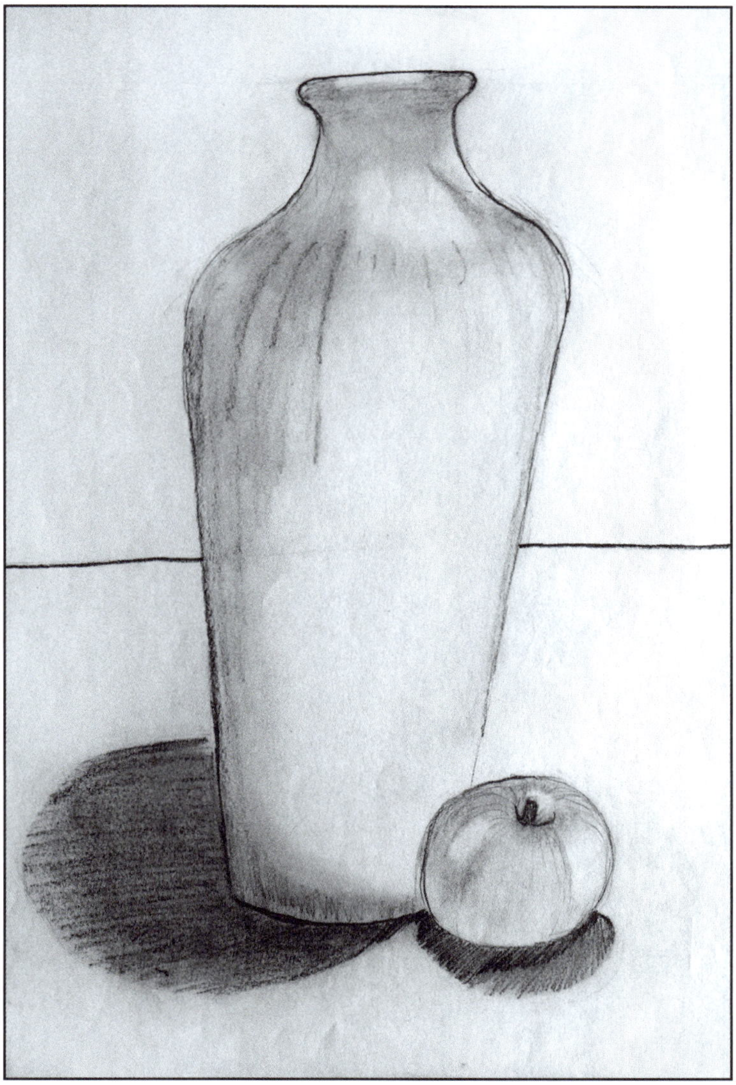

PROJECT 13: Still Life Vase Study – Monochromatic

REVIEW

Monochromatic Color Scheme — A color scheme that uses only tints and/or shades of one color

MATERIALS NEEDED

- ☐ Colored Pencil
- ☐ Pencil
- ☐ Paper
- ☐ Vase
- ☐ Piece of plastic fruit

INSTRUCTIONS

1. Have the students sit in the same place as they sat during the previous lesson. Place the vase and the piece of fruit in the same central location so that students can see it clearly. Have students use a color pencil to draw what they see onto the piece of paper. Again, reinforce and help the students understand proportions. In addition, remind students to use a #2 pencil to create guidelines. (Colored pencil can be difficult to erase.)
2. Have the students determine the light source by determining which way the shadows are cast. Also, remind students how to blend or gradate as they shade to allow for a more three-dimensional look. It is important to remember that when using colored pencil to fill in an object; keep the pencil going in the same direction.

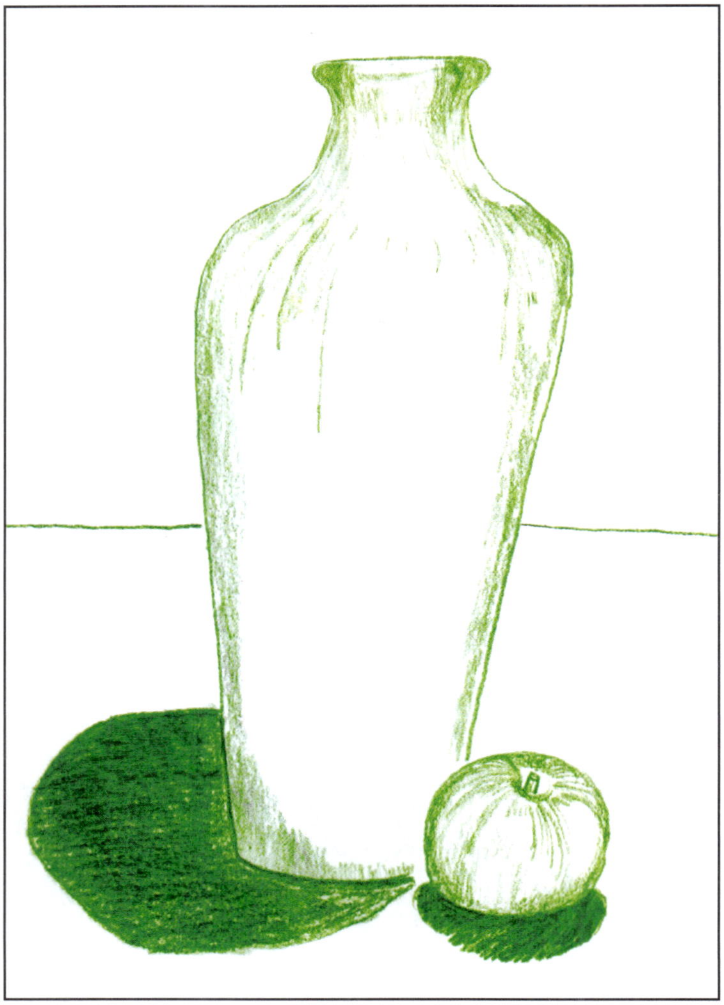

PROJECT 14: Still Life Vase Study – Abstract

REVIEW

Analogous Color Scheme — A color scheme that uses a minimum of two, but no more than five, colors that are adjacent (in a row) on the color wheel

TERMS TO KNOW

Abstract — An image, created through the use of color and shape, that does not represent its original nature

MATERIALS NEEDED

- ☐ Pencil
- ☐ Colored pencils
- ☐ Paper
- ☐ Vase
- ☐ Piece of plastic fruit
- ☐ Ruler

INSTRUCTIONS

1. Have the students sit in the same place as they sat during the previous lesson. Place the vase and the piece of fruit in the same central location so that students can see it clearly. Have students use a #2 pencil to draw what they see on the piece of paper. Again, reinforce and help the students understand proportions. In addition, remind students to use guidelines. This time the students are only outlining their vase and fruit: no shading or shadows.
2. Next, have the students draw 10-16 lines at various angles, both horizontally and vertically, through the entire paper, making sure to darken the table line so it does not blend in with the other lines. (See example below.)
3. Have the students choose a three-color analogous color scheme. Within the vase and fruit only, have the students color each shape a different color, never allowing the same color to touch on a straight line. To explain it differently, no two shapes of the same color may touch on a shared line. For example, two purple shapes may touch each other on a point, but not on a straight line. When you allow two shapes to touch on a straight line, it combines the two shapes and the design of the project is lost.
4. When the students have finished coloring the vase, have them choose a different analogous color scheme and follow the same process with the background <u>below</u> the table line. Remember: If one of the colors was the same as one used on the vase, it cannot touch on the straight line. (See example below.)
5. Lastly, have the students choose a third analogous color scheme and repeat the process for the background <u>above</u> the table line.

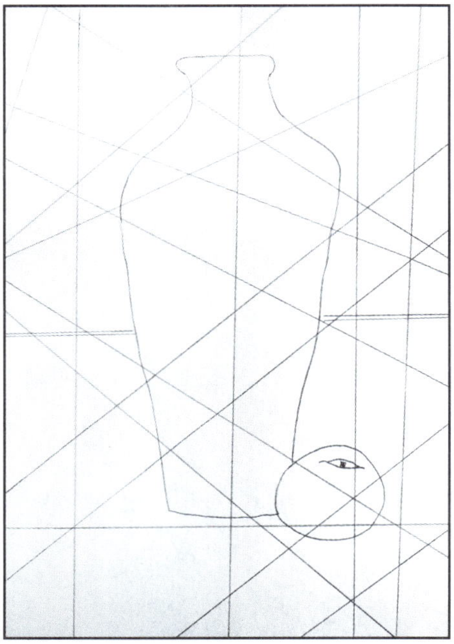

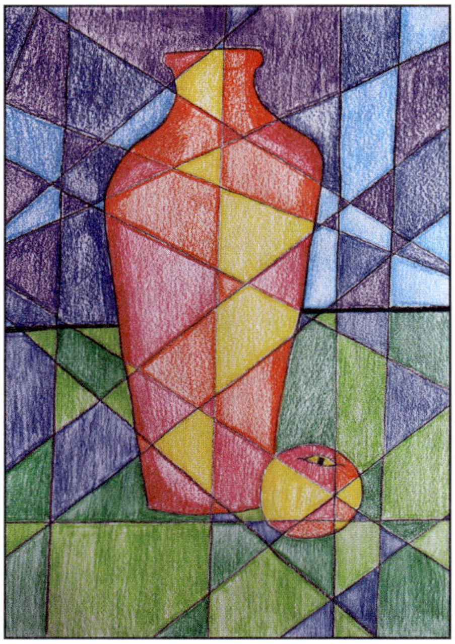

GLOSSARY

Analogous Color Scheme — A color scheme that uses a minimum of two, but no more than five, colors that are adjacent (in a row) on the color wheel. Typically, three colors are used. An example is: R, RO, O.

Background — The far distance

Blending/Gradation — A gentle and gradual transition from dark to light

Bone Tubes — Hollowed-out bones used to store pigment powder

Breathing Area — The space outside the oval

Color Scheme — A fixed relationship between colors and their position on the color wheel

Complementary Color Scheme — A color scheme that uses colors that are directly across from each other on the color wheel: red/green, blue/orange, yellow/violet (purple). Note: Every primary color has a secondary color as a complement.

Continuous Line — A solid line

Continuous Texture — A pattern or image created with smooth, uninterrupted lines (without picking up the pencil, pen, or brush to break the line at any point)

Contrast — The distinction between light colors and dark colors

Crosshatch — Parallel lines that intersect each other, used to shade or mark an image

Curvy Line — A line with soft bends and no angles

Depth — Using objects to give a visual perception, which draws viewers into a picture, or draws their focus to a particular object

Dotted/Dashed Line — A line that is broken into segments or patterns

Foreground — Objects that are close up and in the front (also referred to as the front ground)

Framing — When the foreground, usually a tree or a vine, rises up along the sides to "frame" the subject or focal point

Highlight — A reflection created by a light source

Horizon Line — A line that separates the land/water from the sky

Hue — A color in its natural state, as found on the color wheel

Key Color — Main or predominant color within a project or a piece of art

Landscape View — The format used for landscapes; a rectangle that is wider than it is tall

Landscape — A depiction of the outdoors

Mesopotamia — "Land between two rivers," i.e., the land between the Tigris and Euphrates Rivers

Middle Ground — Usually the focal point of a landscape

Monochromatic Color Scheme — A color scheme that uses only tints and/or shades of one color to create a project or art piece

Mosaic — A picture or design created with small stones or shells

Oval — The space around the subject in a portrait to contain proper proportions. This is not always visible; it is often implied.

Pigment Powder — Colorful powder made from the dust of crushed minerals

Portrait Format — The format used for a portrait; a rectangle that is taller than it is wide

Prehistoric — Before written history

Primary Colors — Colors that cannot be made by mixing other colors: red, yellow, and blue

Sculpture in the Round — A multi-level group of statuettes that signify social standing

Secondary Colors — Colors that are made by mixing two primary colors: orange, green, and violet (purple)

Shade — A natural color to which black has been added to darken it

Split Complementary Color Scheme — A color scheme that uses two colors directly adjacent (on either side of) to the complement of the key color. Example: If red is the key color, then its complement is green and the split complementary color scheme is: R, YG, BG.

Standard — A banner or flag

Still Life — A prearranged group of inanimate objects with contrasting textures; usually includes fruits, flowers, glass, or ceramics

Stipple/Dot — A texture, picture, or image created with dots

Tertiary Color — A color created by mixing together one primary and one adjacent secondary color

Tint — A natural color to which white has been added to lighten it

Triad Color Scheme — Using three colors equally spaced on the color wheel

Value — The relative lightness or darkness of a color; also referred to as gray scale

Visual Spectrum — The range of wavelengths the human eye can see

Zigzag — A combination of diagonal lines that connect at each point

TEMPLATES

COLOR WHEEL

Name: ______________________________ **Date:** ______________

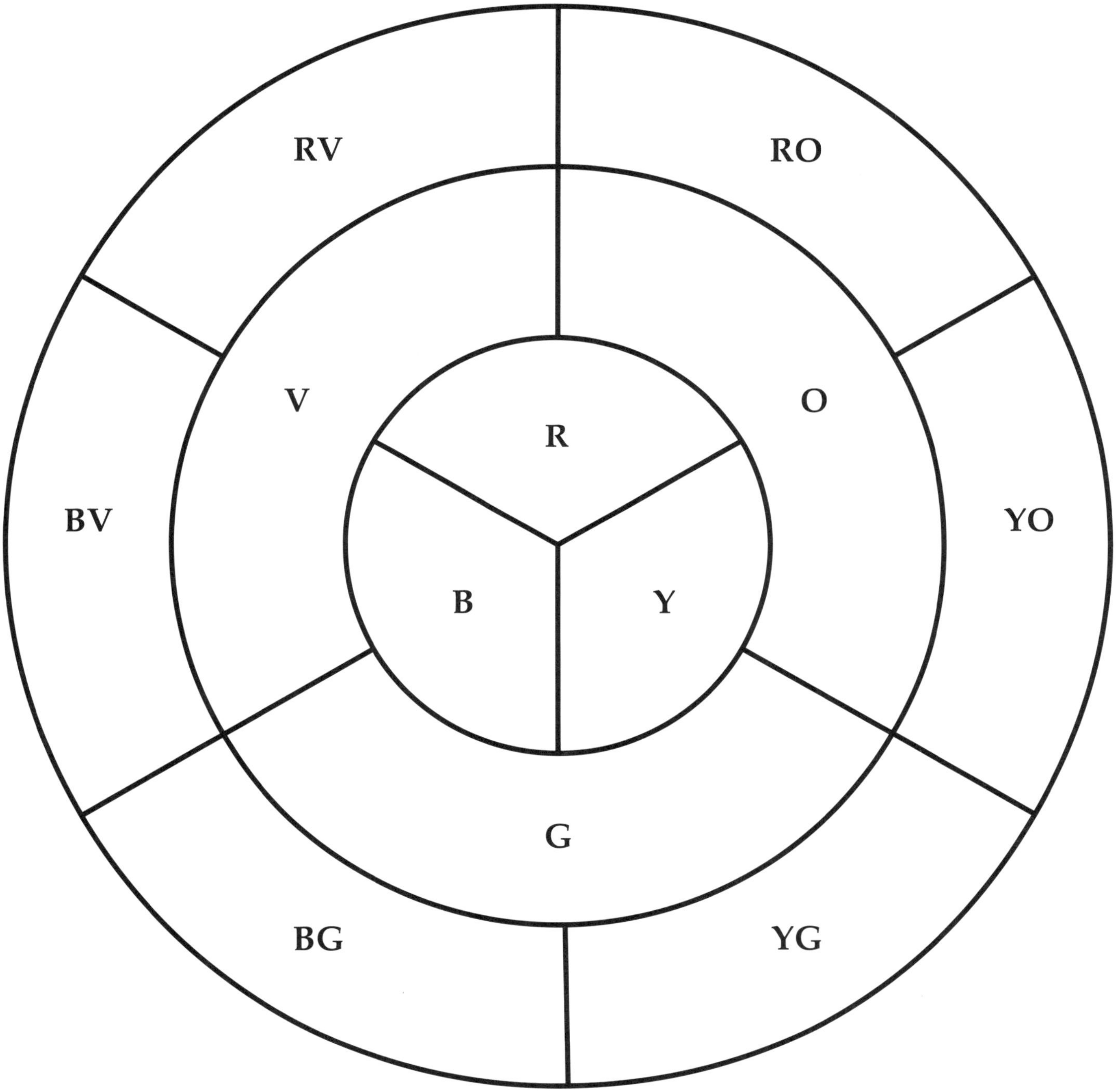

PROJECT 4A: Scarecrow Template

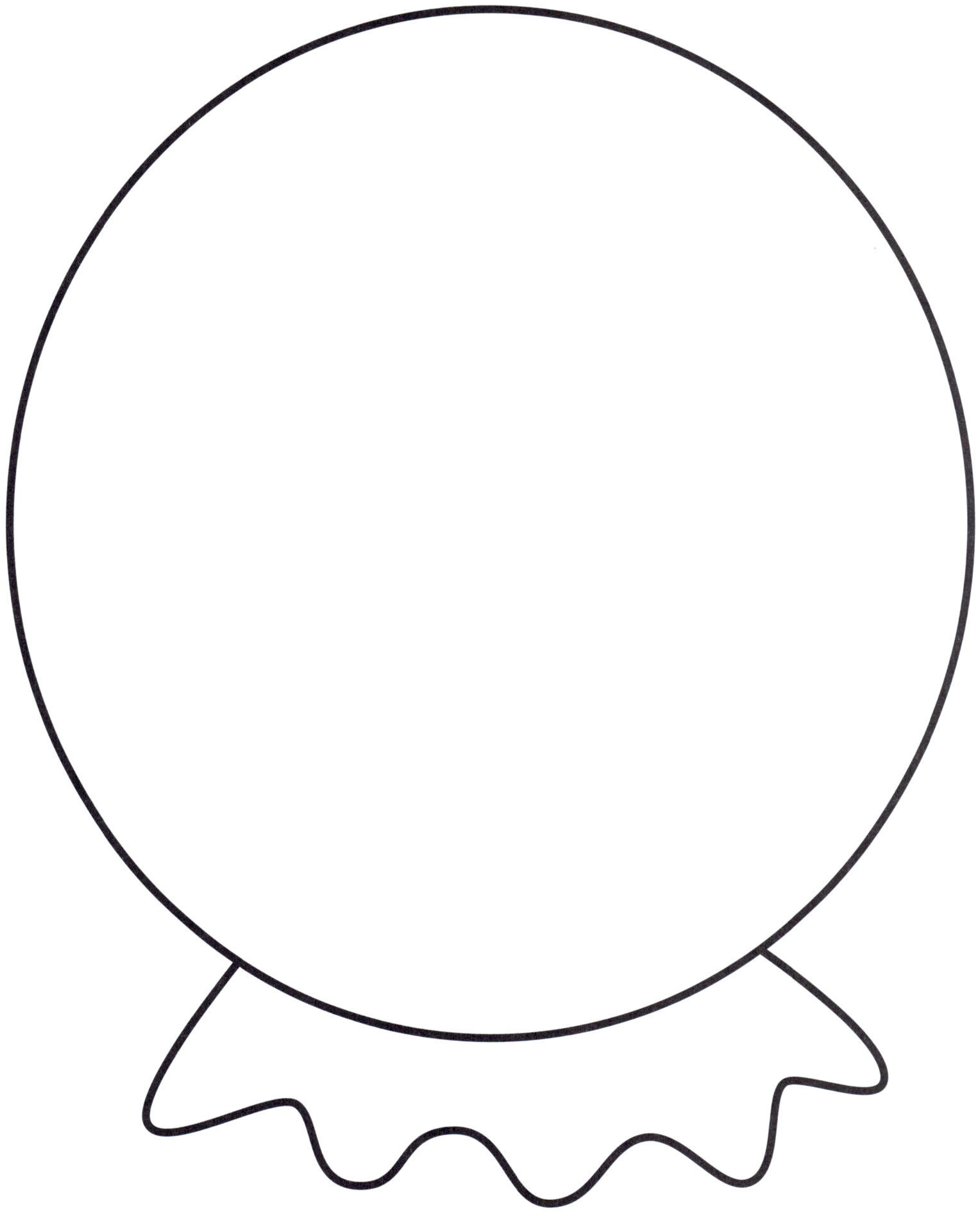

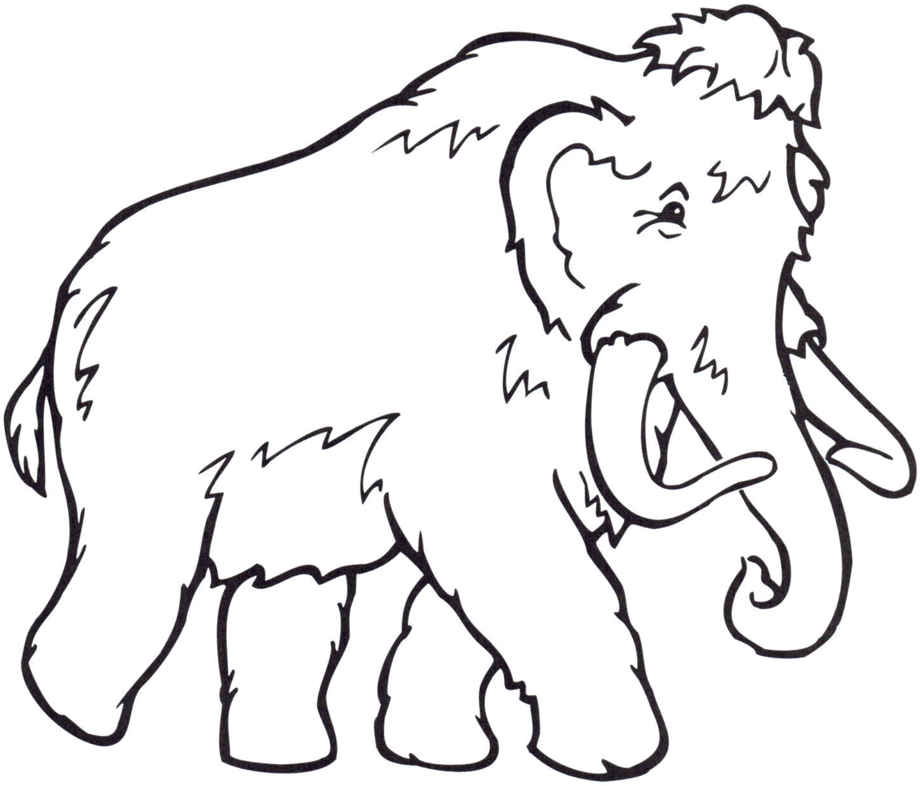

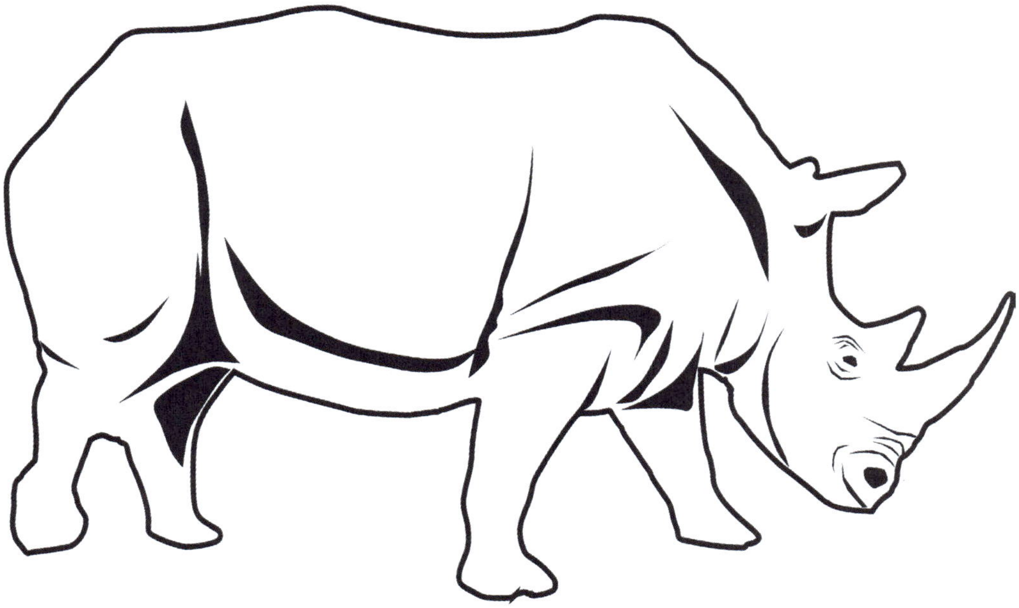

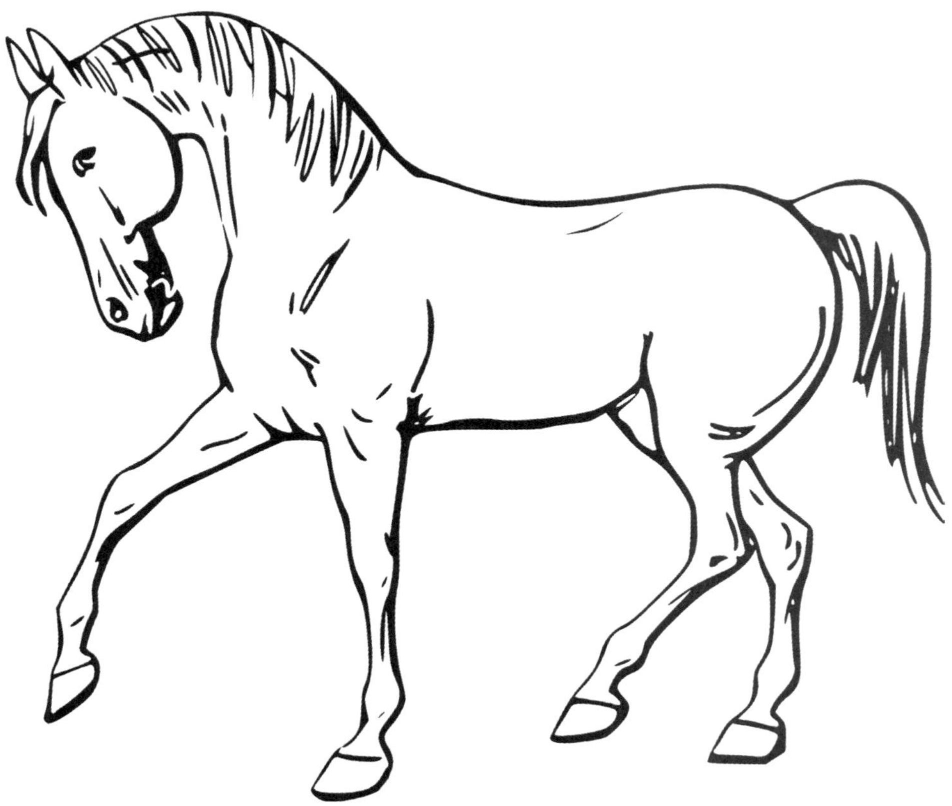

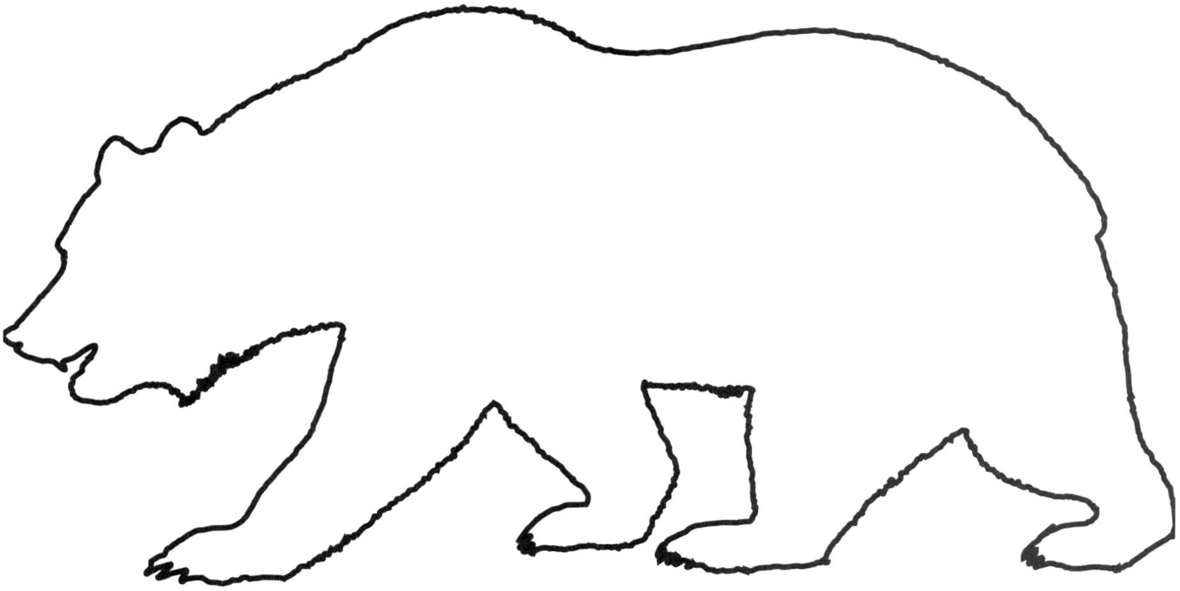

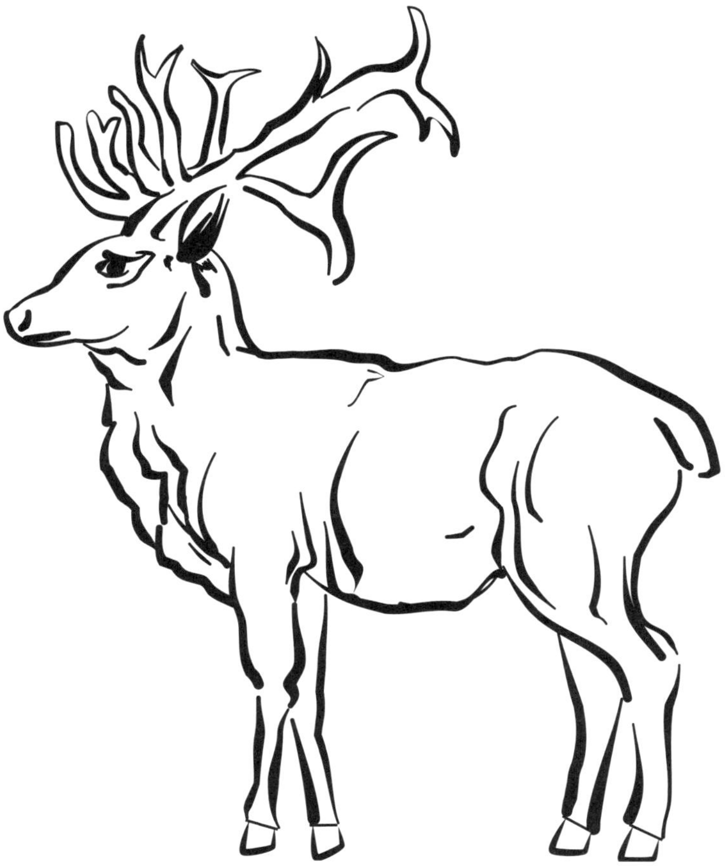

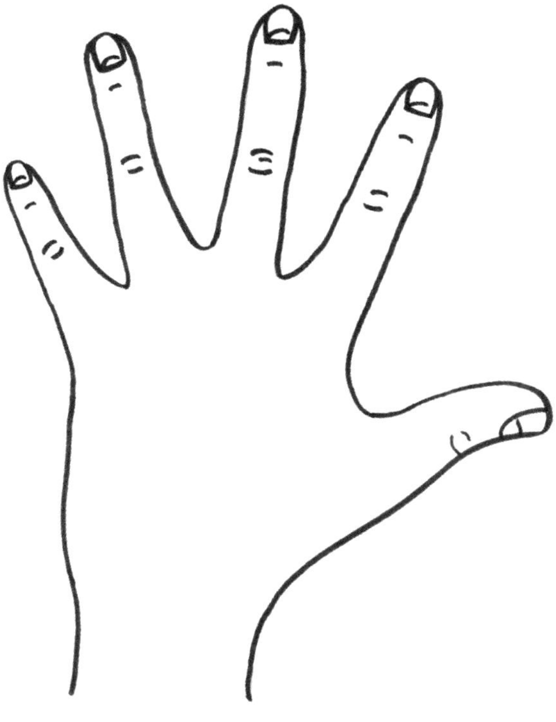

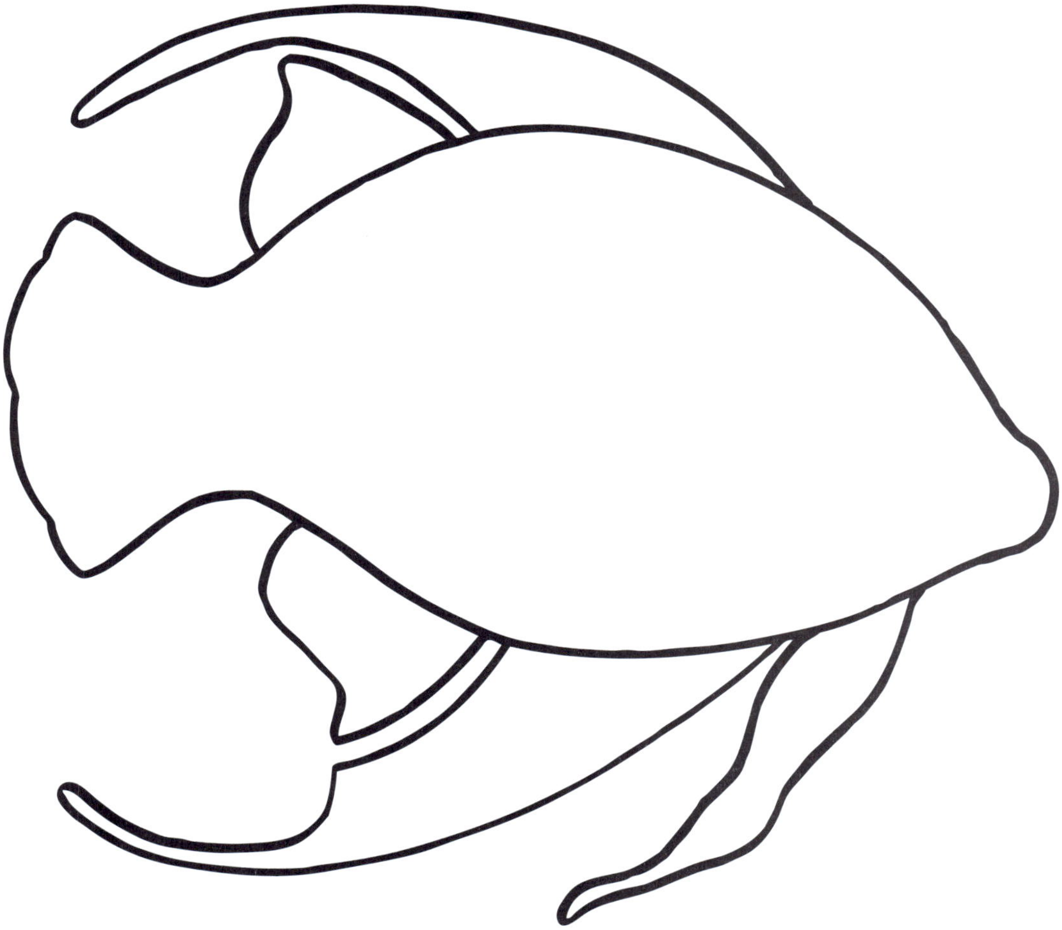

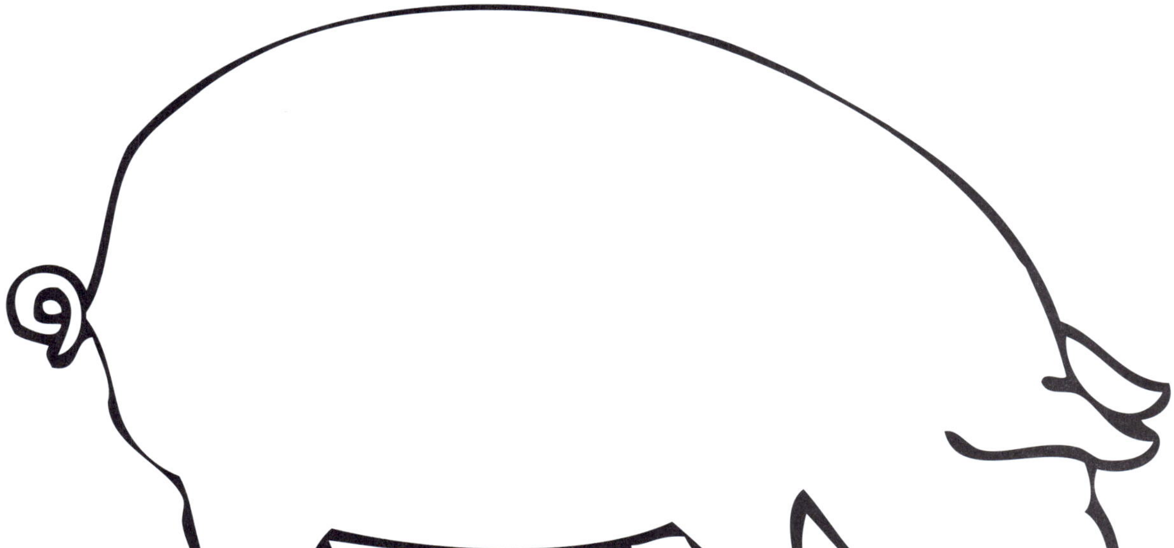

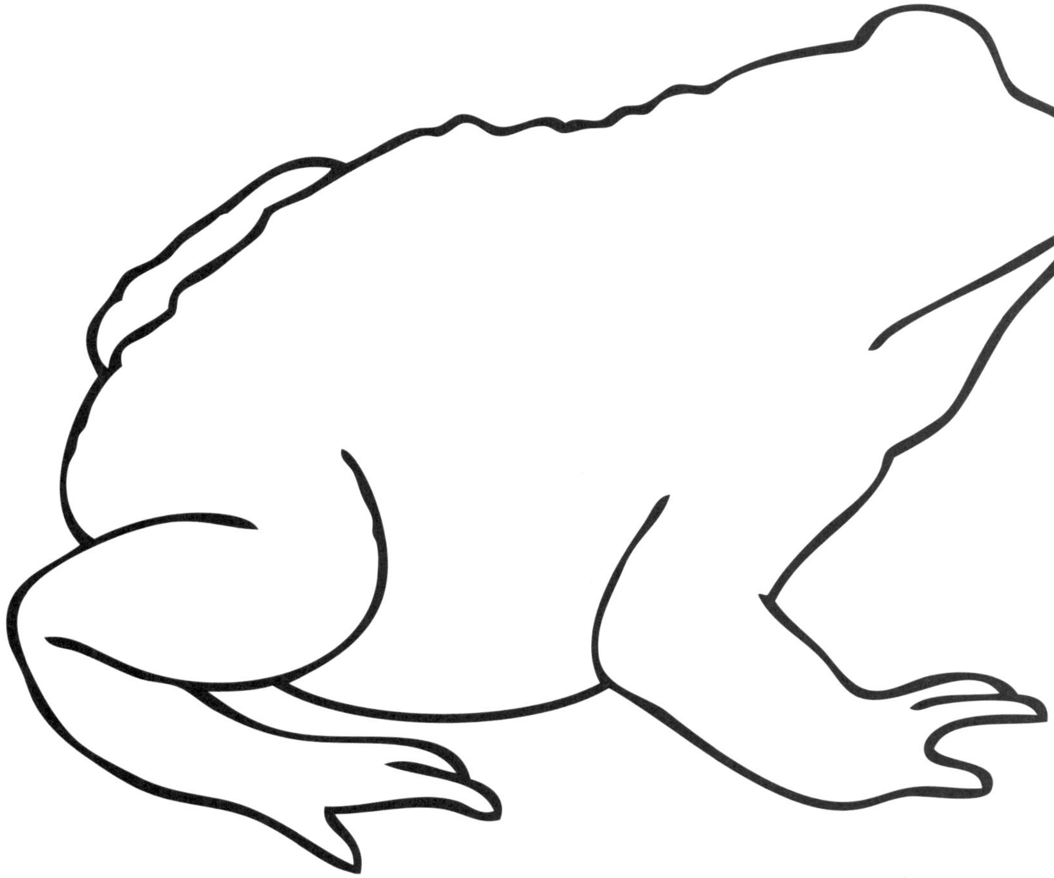

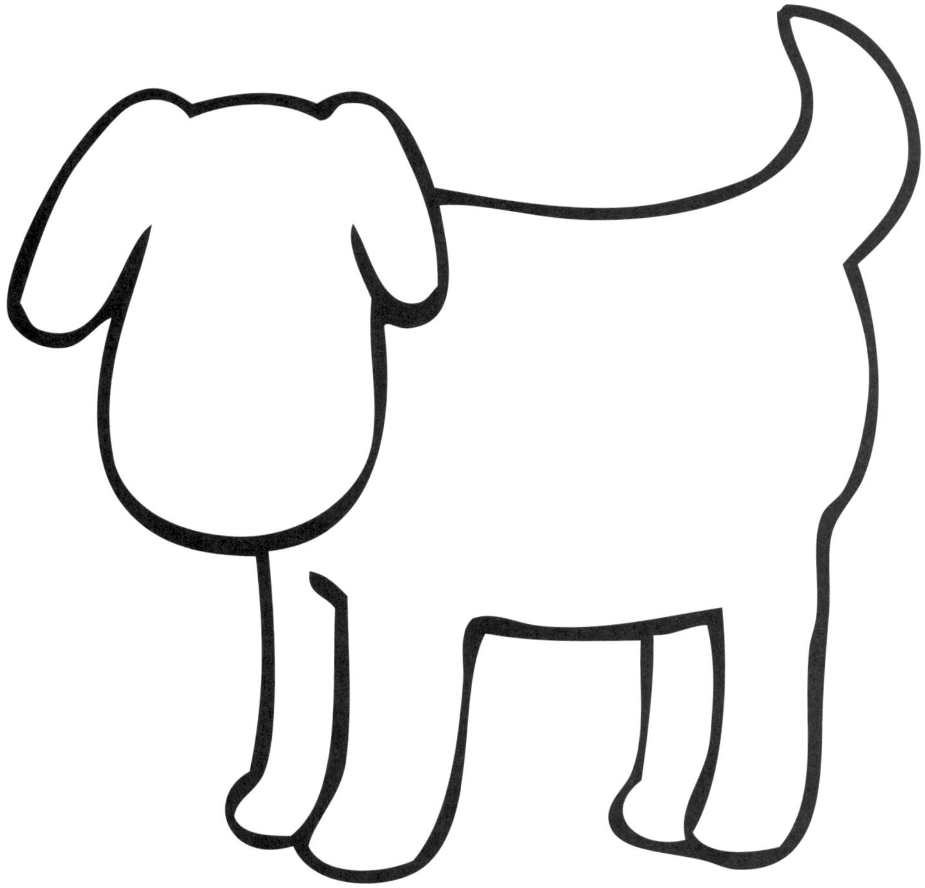

QUIZZES

COLOR AND LINE QUIZ

Name:____ Date: ________________ Score: _______

Please circle the correct answer below each definition.

1. Colors that come from mixing a primary color with a secondary color directly adjacent on the color wheel with the primary color listed first.
   a. Complementary color **b.** Tertiary color **c.** Visible spectrum

2. Adding black to a color.
   a. Shade **b.** Tint **c.** Contrast

3. Using any 2 colors directly opposite from each other on the color wheel.
   a. Monochromatic **b.** Complementary **c.** Analogous

4. Using colors that are adjacent (in a row) on the color wheel. (Using a min. of 2 and a max. of 5. Typically in groups of 3.)
   a. Monochromatic **b.** Complementary **c.** Analogous

5. Draw and name the 3 line directions below: (2 pts. per answer)

   1.

   2.

   3.

6. Name three line types below.

   1. __________________________________

   2. __________________________________

   3. __________________________________

7. Draw an example of each texture listed below:

   1. Stipple

   2. Crosshatch

Bonus Question: What is another name for the gray scale? __________________________________

PORTRAIT AND LANDSCAPE QUIZ

Name:____ Date: _________________ Score: _______

1. Label each portrait (Profile, ¾ view, Full Face) (3 pts.)

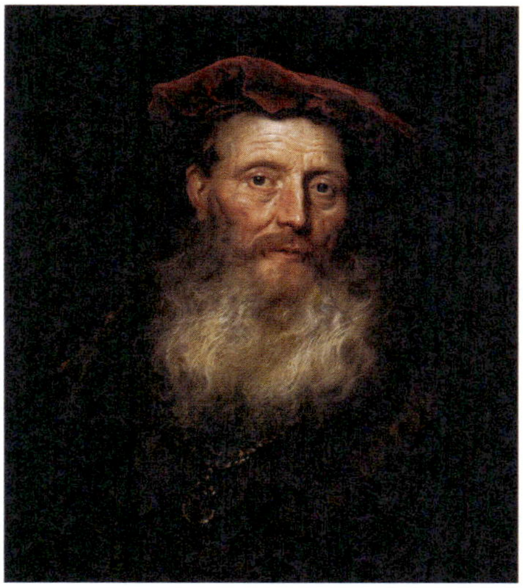

Bearded Man with a Velvet Cap by Govert Flinck

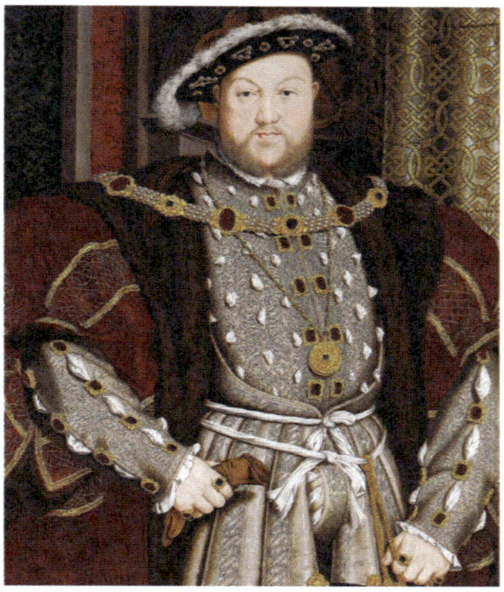

Portrait of Henry VIII by Hans Holbein the Younger

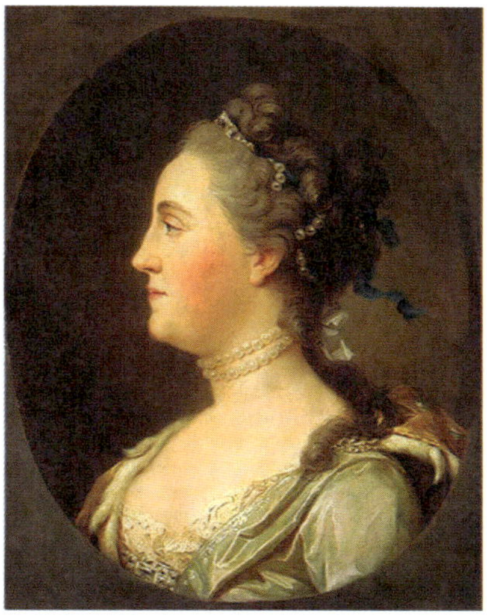

Portrait of Catherine II by Vigilius Eriksen

__________________________ __________________________ __________________________

2. Label the portrait with the terms below. Then identify its *length (½ length, ¾ length or full length).* (3 pts.)

a. Breathing area **b.** Subject

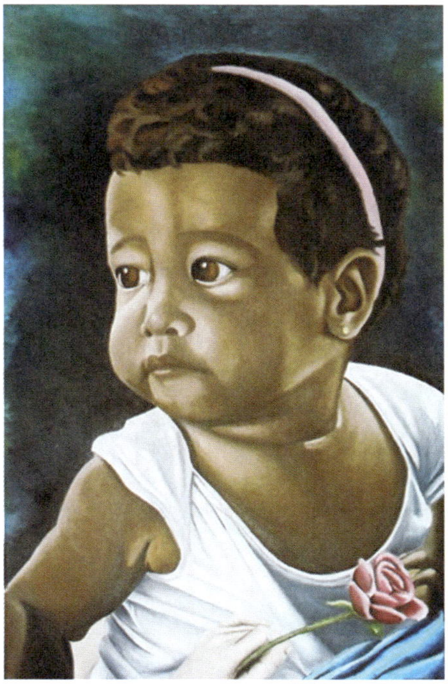

Venezuelan Baby by Jocelyn Albright

Length: ________________________

3. Label the landscape with the following terms below. (5 pts.)
   a. Foreground b. Background c. Middle ground d. Horizon line e. Framing

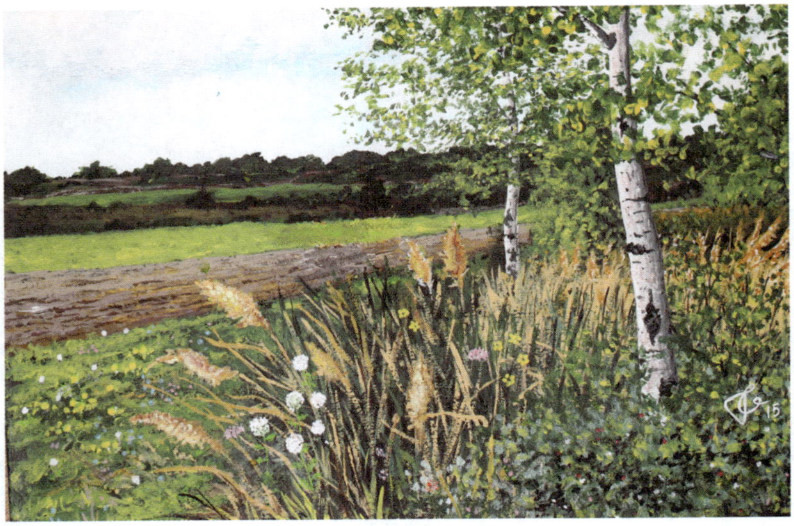

Painting by Tom Greenslade

True or False (1 pt. ea.)

_________ 4. Landscapes are a depiction of an outdoor scene.

_________ 5. Long Rectangle is the most common type of landscape and is taller than it is wide.

_________ 6. The background is usually less detailed and blurry.

7. Label the horizon line on this perspective.

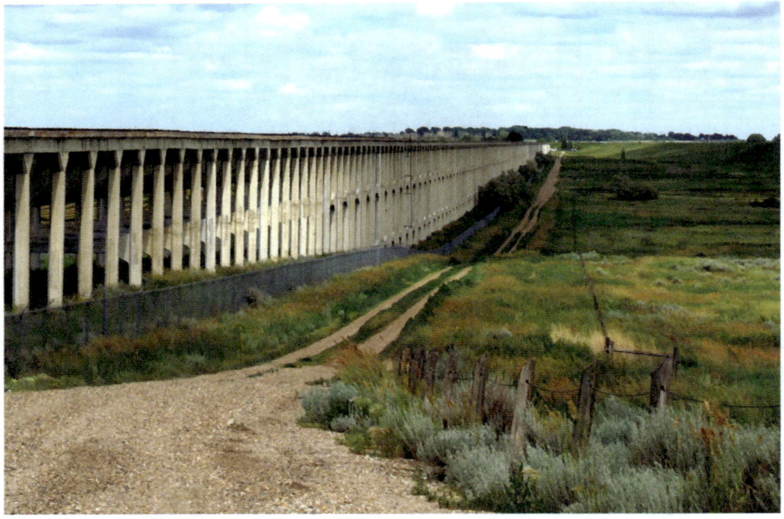

Based on photo of Brooks Aqueduct by Darryl Darwent (CC BY 2.0)

Bonus Questions:

1. Name the 3 line ***directions***: ____

2. What is a monochromatic color scheme?____________________________________

____

PRE-HISTORIC ART QUIZ

Name:______________________________ Date: ______________ Score: ________

Please circle the correct answers.

1. What does prehistoric mean?
   a. Before written history b. Before time began c. When HLS was started

2. Which group of animals are some of the most common painted in caves?
   a. lions, tigers, bears b. stags, bulls, mammoths c. horses, dogs, fish

3. Which group of Tools where used to Paint in caves?
   a. bones, feathers, hair b. rollers, brushes c. sticks, stones

4. What is the pigment powder used for?
   a. baking b. cleaning c. painting

5. What is pigment powder stored in?
   a. jars b. bone tubes c. leather sacs

6. Black paint was made from which item?
   a. burned bones b. caulk c. magnesium

7. Yellow paint was made from which item?
   a. limestone b. ocher c. calcite

8. Cave paintings were signed using what?
   a. footprints b. handprints c. fingerprints

9. Which color was not used for cave paintings?
   a. white b. purple c. orange

10. Cave paintings have been found on which continent?
    a. Antarctica b. Asia c. Australia

Bonus Questions:

1. What is the area outside the oval in a portrait called? ______________________

2. Name the three complementary color schemes.

   1. ______________________
   2. ______________________
   3. ______________________

MESOPOTAMIAN QUIZ

Name:____ Date: ________________ Score: ________

Please circle the correct answers.

1. What does Mesopotamia mean?
   a. Land between 2 rivers   b. Land without water   c. Land between the sea

2. In a "sculpture in the round," which figure is less powerful?
   a. The servant   b. The worshiper   c. The priest

3. What does the word standard?
   a. rules of life   b. banner/flag   c. requirements

4. What is a mosaic?
   a. Carved wood with ivory   b. Small pieces that make a picture   c. Statue with a beard

5. What is a cylinder seal?
   a. A small carved cylinder stone   b. A small cylinder animal statue   c. A cylinder wax stamp

True or False

________ 1. A mosaic is a picture made from small stones and shells.

________ 2. A standard tells a story through words and pictures.

________ 3. A ziggurat is a temple in a pyramid-type shape.

________ 4. A sculpture in the round is made up of small statues in rows.

________ 5. Mesopotamia is between the Euphrates and the Tigris Rivers.

Bonus Questions:

1. What are the 3 sections of a landscape?

   1. ________________________________

   2. ________________________________

   3. ________________________________

2. Name 2 complementary color schemes.

   1. ________________________________

   2. ________________________________

EGYPTIAN QUIZ

Name:____ Date: ________________ Score: _______

Please circle the correct answers.

1. What are hieroglyphics?
   - **a.** Egyptian letters
   - **b.** Egyptian jewelry
   - **c.** Egyptian buildings
2. What is a cartouche?
   - **a.** A form of transportation
   - **b.** A name plate
   - **c.** an Egyptian bug
3. The lids of Canopic jars resemble the four sons of Horus and are represented by which beings?
   - **a.** Human, falcon, baboon, dog
   - **b.** Human, dog, lion, eagle
   - **c.** Human, falcon, beetle, worm
4. What is a scarab?
   - **a.** A large dessert beetle
   - **b.** A symbol of great power
   - **c.** A figure of Egyptian mythology
   - **d.** All of the above
5. What is a cylinder seal?
   - **a.** A small carved cylinder stone
   - **b.** A small cylinder animal statue
   - **c.** A cylinder wax stamp

True or False

________ **1.** The Rosetta Stone was the key to understanding hieroglyphics.

________ **2.** A register tells a story through hieroglyphics and pictures.

________ **3.** Hieroglyphics represent words and meanings.

________ **4.** A pectoral is a large ornate necklace worn over the chest.

________ **5.** Egypt was divided into two kingdoms, lower and upper Egypt.

Bonus Questions:

1. What are the 3 symbols of Lower Egypt?

1. ________________________________

2. ________________________________

3. ________________________________

2. Name 2 secondary colors.

1. ________________________________

2. ________________________________

COLOR AND LINE QUIZ – Answer Key

Name:______________________________ Date: ______________ Score: ________

Please circle the correct answer below each definition.

1. Colors that come from mixing a primary color with a secondary color directly adjacent on the color wheel with the primary color listed first.
  a. Complementary color **b.** Tertiary color **c.** Visible spectrum

2. Adding black to a color.
  a. Shade **b.** Tint **c.** Contrast

3. Using any 2 colors directly opposite from each other on the color wheel.
  a. Monochromatic **b.** Complementary **c.** Analogous

4. Using colors that are adjacent (in a row) on the color wheel. (Using a min. of 2 and a max. of 5. Typically in groups of 3.)
  a. Monochromatic **b.** Complementary **c.** Analogous

5. **Draw** and **name** the three ***line directions*** below: (2 pts. per answer)

  1. Vertical **2.** Horizontal **3.** Diagonal

6. Name three ***line types*** below.

  1. Continuous **2.** Dashed/Dotted **3.** Curved or Zigzag

7. Draw an example of each texture listed below:

  1. Stipple

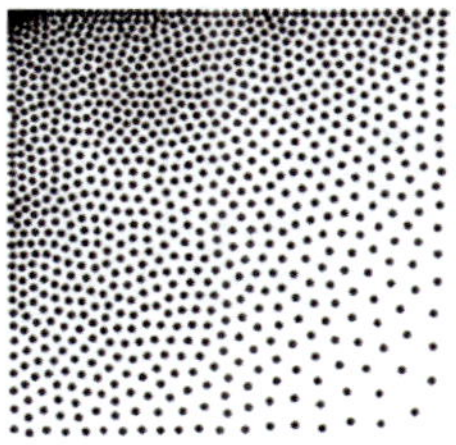

  2. Crosshatch

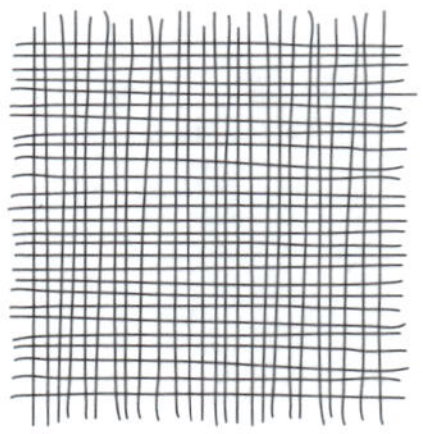

Bonus Question: What is another name for the gray scale? Value Scale

PORTRAIT AND LANDSCAPE QUIZ – Answer Key

Name:______________________________ Date: ______________ Score: ________

1. Label each portrait (Profile, ¾ view, Full Face) (3 pts.)

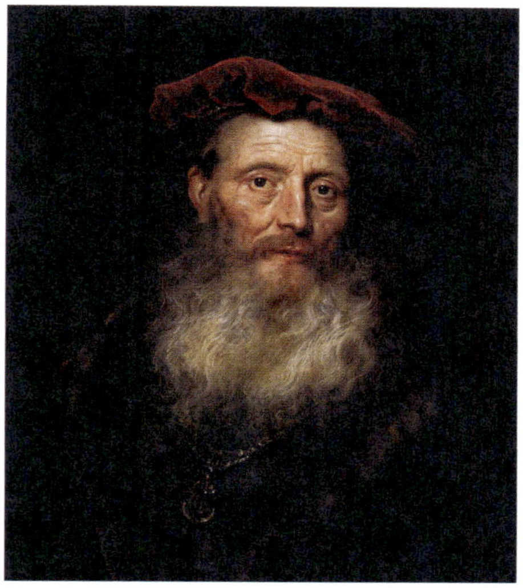

Bearded Man with a Velvet Cap by Govert Flinck

3/4 view

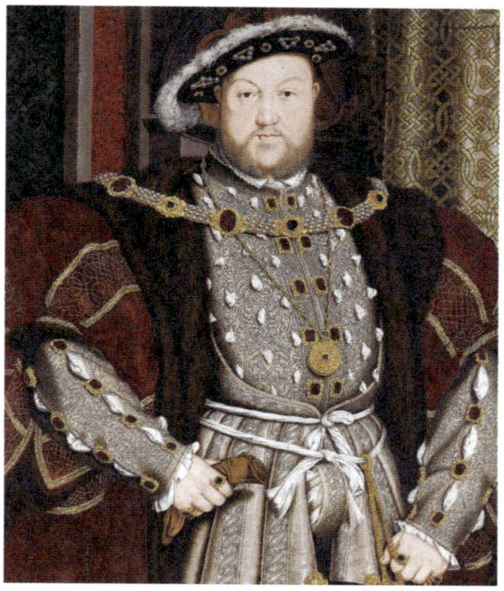

Portrait of Henry VIII by Hans Holbein the Younger

Full Face

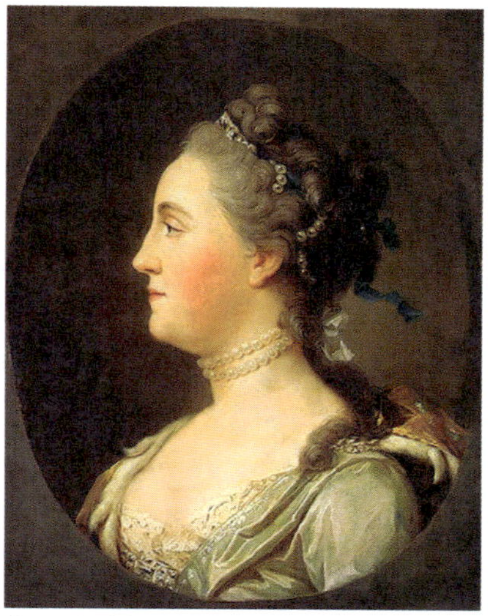

Portrait of Catherine II by Vigilius Eriksen

Profile

2. Label the portrait with the terms below. Then identify its *length (½ length, ¾ length or full length)*. (3 pts.)
   a. Breathing area **b.** Subject

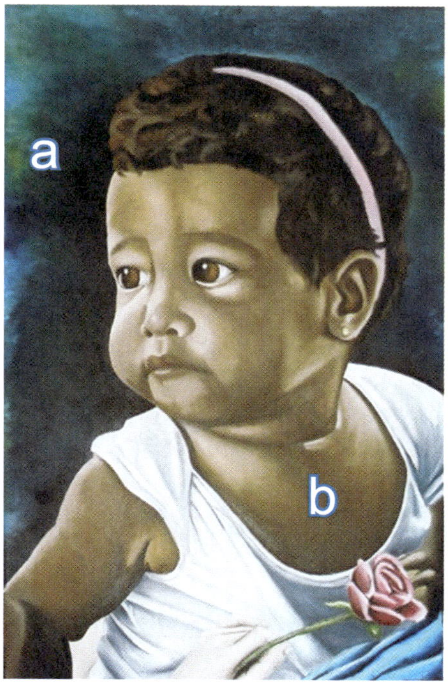

Venezuelan Baby by Jocelyn Albright

Length: 1/2 length

3. Label the landscape with the following terms below. (5 pts.)
   a. Foreground   b. Background   c. Middle ground   d. Horizon line   e. Framing

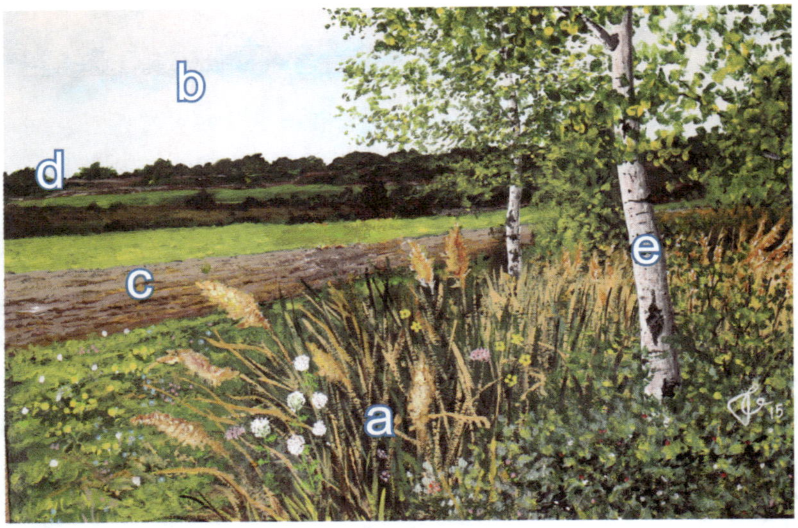

Painting by Tom Greenslade

True or False (1 pt. ea.)

___T___ 4. Landscapes are a depiction of an outdoor scene.

___F___ 5. Long Rectangle is the most common type of landscape and is taller than it is wide.

___T___ 6. The background is usually less detailed and blurry.

7. Label the horizon line on this perspective.

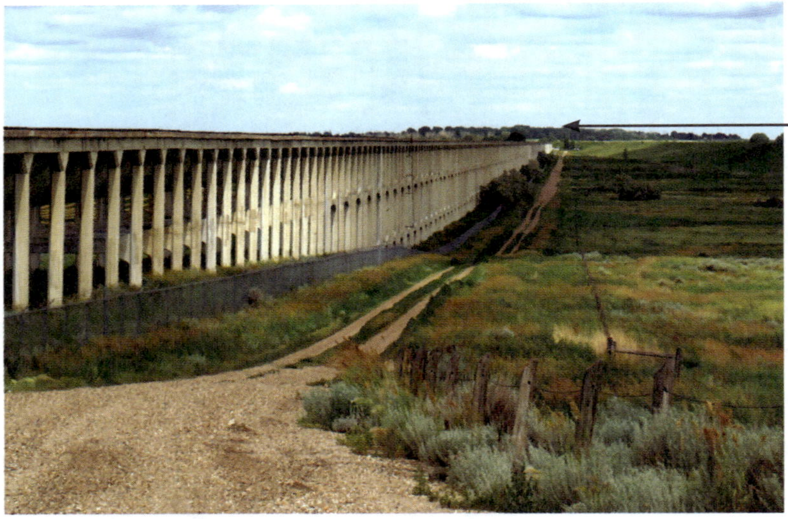

horizon line

Based on photo of Brooks Aqueduct by Darryl Darwent (CC BY 2.0)

Bonus Questions:

1. Name the 3 line ***directions***: vertical, horizontal, diagonal

2. What is a monochromatic color scheme?
   A color scheme that uses only tints and/or shades of one color.

PRE-HISTORIC ART QUIZ – Answer Key

Name:______________________________ Date: ______________ Score: ________

Please circle the correct answers.

1. What does prehistoric mean?
   a. Before written History b. Before time began c. When HLS was started
2. Which group of animals are some of the most common painted in caves?
   a. lions, tigers, bears b. stags, bulls, mammoths c. horses, dogs, fish
3. Which group of Tools where used to paint in caves?
   a. bones, feathers, hair b. rollers, brushes c. sticks, stones
4. What is the pigment powder used for?
   a. baking b. cleaning c. painting
5. What is pigment powder stored in?
   a. jars b. bone tubes c. leather sacs
6. Black paint was made from which item?
   a. burned bones b. caulk c. magnesium
7. Yellow paint was made from which item?
   a. limestone b. ocher c. calcite
8. Cave paintings were signed using what?
   a. footprints b. handprints c. fingerprints
9. Which color was not used for cave paintings?
   a. white b. purple c. orange
10. Cave paintings have been found on which continent?
    a. Antarctica b. Asia c. Australia

Bonus Questions:

1. What is the area outside the oval in a portrait called? Breathing Area
2. Name the three complementary color schemes.
   1. Blue/Orange
   2. Red/Green
   3. Yellow/Purple

MESOPOTAMIAN QUIZ – Answer Key

Name:______________________________ Date: ______________ Score: ______

Please circle the correct answers.

1. What does Mesopotamia mean?
   a. Land between 2 rivers b. Land without water c. Land between the sea
2. In a "sculpture in the round," which figure is less powerful?
   a. The servant b. The worshiper c. The priest
3. What does the word standard mean?
   a. Rules of life b. Banner/Flag c. Requirements
4. What is a mosaic?
   a. Carved wood with Ivory b. Small pieces that make a picture c. Statue with a beard
5. What is a cylinder seal?
   a. A small carved cylinder stone b. A small cylinder animal statue c. A cylinder wax stamp

True or False

__T__ 1. A mosaic is a picture made from small stones and shells.

__F__ 2. A standard tells a story through words and pictures.

__T__ 3. A ziggurat is a temple in a pyramid-type shape.

__T__ 4. A sculpture in the round is made up of small statues in rows.

__T__ 5. Mesopotamia is between the Euphrates and the Tigris Rivers.

Bonus Questions:

1. What are the 3 sections of a landscape?
   1. Foreground
   2. Middle Ground
   3. Background
2. Name 2 complementary color schemes.
   1. red/green, blue/orange, or yellow/purple
   2. ____________________

EGYPTIAN QUIZ – Answer Key

Name:______________________ Date: ____________ Score: ______

Please circle the correct answers.

1. What are hieroglyphics?
   a. Egyptian letters
   b. Egyptian jewelry
   c. Egyptian buildings
2. What is a cartouche?
   a. A form of transportation
   b. A name plate
   c. an Egyptian bug
3. The lids of Canopic jars resemble the four sons of Horus and are represented by which beings?
   a. Human, falcon, baboon, dog
   b. Human, dog, lion, eagle
   c. Human, falcon, beetle, worm
4. What is a scarab?
   a. A large dessert beetle
   b. A symbol of great power
   c. A figure of Egyptian mythology
   d. All of the above
5. What is a cylinder seal?
   a. A small carved cylinder stone
   b. A small cylinder animal statue
   c. A cylinder wax stamp

True or False

T 1. The Rosetta Stone was the key to understanding hieroglyphics.

T 2. A register tells a story through hieroglyphics and pictures.

F 3. Hieroglyphics represent words and meanings.

T 4. A pectoral is a large ornate necklace worn over the chest.

T 5. Egypt was divided into two kingdoms, Lower and Upper Egypt.

Bonus Questions:

1. What are the 3 symbols of Lower Egypt?
   1. Papyrus plant
   2. Red crown
   3. cobra
2. Name 2 secondary colors.
   1. green, orange, or purple
   2. ____________